Moving
Pros

**The must-have
guide for
anyone thinking
about relocating
to Florida.**

Includes cost of
living, how to move,
real estate & property
in Florida basics

Dagny Wasil

BookSpecs Publishing
Pennsville, New Jersey

Moving to Florida
– Pros & Cons

By Dagny Wasil

Published by: BookSpecs Publishing, 16 Sunset Ave., Pennsville, NJ 08070, 856-678-2186

ISBN 978-0-9903276-2-2

LCCN 2014941067

Table of Contents

INTRODUCTION

For some people, moving to Florida is the perfect choice. It's a match seemingly made in heaven. The love the weather, the outdoor activities the new friends and the new lifestyle found in the Sunshine State.

For others, coming to Florida is like a whirlwind relationship. It begins with love at first sight. They gaze at the beautiful fruit and flowers and palms. Then they bask in the laid-back atmosphere or lively nightlife (depending upon their personal preferences). At some point, with their feet in the sand or lounging beneath the generous sun, they confess their love. They convince themselves they can't live another day if they don't live it in Florida!

They begin making plans. They start answering their own questions: Where will I (or "we") move? When? What will I do upon arrival? How will time be spent? What lifestyle will be embraced? Soon afterwards, these people have sold everything, packed their bags and moved halfway across the country to be in the state they adore.

But after a period of months, when the new wears off, those same folks begin seeing things they hadn't noticed before. They may get frustrated spending hours on end in winter traffic (when the State's population doubles from the arrival of visitors up north). Or they are evacuated from their homes a couple of times (during summer) in order to evade oncoming hurricanes. They begin tapping into hard-earned life savings in order to pay for things like flood insurance and electric bills. And so on.

After that, they begin really disliking other things: The frequent muggy weather, the bugs, certain overcrowded beaches, etc. They realize they never really loved Florida at all. They only loved what they thought she was. By then, they find themselves making a choice they would never have imagined before their arrival. They decide to leave.

And leave they do, often at great expense. At one point, just a few years ago, almost three-quarters of the people who had moved to Florida with high hopes and aspiring dreams found themselves leaving it behind.

Many times it's because these folks had no idea what they were in for after making Florida their permanent home. Like a young, impressionable lover, their eyes were too focused on the positives to consider the whole picture and they had no idea what they in for after making the move to this lovely, albeit sometimes challenging, place.

These are the types of people I want to talk to. I want to help open everyone's eyes to some things about Florida they probably didn't experience on vacation or find while researching the Internet. I want to help them explore questions like, "Do I really want to move away from everything I know and love?" "Will I really be happy with the warm weather?" "Can I actually afford to live in Florida?"

Florida can be both wonderful and breathtakingly beautiful at times. But an old friend once said to me, "You can't eat pretty."

Let this book serve as a tool to help you move past the Florida razzle dazzle to a fully informed choice. Many full-time residents absolutely love this place. But I'd like for your decision to move here to be a sound one, as opposed to a completely emotional one. That way, you're much more likely to decide what really is best for you.

AGES AND STAGES

Because of Florida's lure, its people make up a unique age demographic that affects the state's pace and economy. Here are a few things you might to consider, depending on what stage of life you're in.

Young People...

According to U.S. Census estimates for 2012, about 20 percent of the population of Florida is under the age of 18, with 5 percent of those being below school age. Although that number is only a few points lower than the national average, it does affect some things.

Instead of Florida neighborhoods teaming with children, most residents have children that are grown and out of the house. This means in many areas, friends may be hard to come by for little ones and teenagers.

The quality of Florida public schools has also been a problem in recent decades. Although in the past five years, Florida has risen from thirty-first place to fifth, according to Education Week's national school rankings. For parents of publicly-schooled children in Florida there is always a concern students may not have access to high-performing teachers or technologies.

Almost 76 percent of high school students graduate, which is a number very similar to the national average. But actual quality of education, rather than pieces of paper, is far more important.

Senior Citizens...

On the other end of the spectrum are the over 65 group, who make up more than 18 percent of the population. That number is about 5 percent more than the national average.

Most of these individuals are retired and have come to Florida to enjoy the easy pace of life. This slower pace also has a tendency to slow down the pace for the rest of Florida too, which occasionally shows up in traffic or grocery store lines.

Economically, the burden of such a large amount of residents not participating in the labor force, yet collecting Medicaid, puts Florida in a unique situation. It pays out the fifth largest amounts for Medicaid in the nation but ranks in the bottom five on how much it spends per person. As the need for Medicaid grows, that money will have to come from somewhere.

Somewhere in Between...

For the other 62 percent of Floridians, Florida represents diverse age groups and opportunities. This is especially true when it comes to making money. Florida's unemployment rates are, at the time of this writing, back in the single digits. They're no longer among the highest in the country. There are more jobs, but they may not be what a worker necessarily wants to do.

Between retirees and tourism, the demand for low-skilled workers in service industries is higher. Finding a good paying job, however, isn't going to be as easy as it might be somewhere else. As of January 2014, minimum wage was $7.93 per hour, but it's challenging to maintain a home with low income.

Many homeowners have found their living expenses cannot be maintained on the wages they make in Florida. Those having a Bachelors' degree, or above, may receive higher wages, but the competition is stiffer.

Coastal Culture...

Although overall pace of Florida is slow, the west coast and keys move even slower. In these areas, there is very much an island mindset where times are approximate and everything can wait until tomorrow.

If you're ready to retire, this atmosphere may be conducive to the R&R you are looking for. As for young people, couples with young children, or older adults just hitting their stride, neither the pace nor the economic opportunities in Florida might match expectations or desires. These are all important realties one should consider before moving to Florida.

HEART AND HOME

Moving to Florida might involve packing up and moving halfway across the country. If transplanting to Florida is going to be the biggest move of your life, it might be wise to consider whether the sunny days and beaches will outweigh the emotions of leaving your family, friends and current everyday routines behind.

The word homesick might conjure up childhood memories of your first week of camp or your first year of college. But adults get homesick too. So much so that it's now recognized as the deciding factor for many people for whether they decide to stay in Florida or not.

The list below may help determine if you'll be able to handle familial ties and other separation before moving to Florida. After all, you do want to avoid any potential hassle and expense of moving right back to where you originally came from.

What You'll Leave Behind...
Let's take a few moments and discuss those things you're going to be leaving behind. At first, many folks think they want to escape these things. But after a short period in the Sunshine State they begin regretting the changes they had first imagined would bring them happiness. They

come to see that the changes in lifestyle now available to them aren't what they really wanted after all. What changes are we talking about here?

Your Community...

Have you lived in the same area for most of your life? If you have, you most likely know all the best resources within your community.

You know the best stores to get shoes, the best restaurants, and perhaps even the best golf courses (if that is your hobby). You may know where the friendliest waiters and convenience store clerks are. You also probably know about annual events, free concerts, and local plays — all little things that give you the "insider's view" of your town and surrounding areas.

Your community may even contain the house you grew up in, the church you got married in, or the park you brought your young children to when they were very small. It may be packed with pleasant memories of festivals and holidays.

Once you move, all the familiar things about your community (that you really liked) will be replaced with unfamiliar. Everything in your environment will look and feel different. People may react differently to you. Your family or close friends may not be minutes away anymore.

Of course, you might think after vacationing in Florida that you'll like these differences. Remember, however, that things which may have been thrilling on vacation will seem a lot different when you're a new resident in a place you know very little about.

Four Seasons...

For a lot of people, Florida's lure is the mild-to-warm temperatures. Daytime temperatures in most areas range from mid to high 60s in the winter months to high 80s in the summer (Fahrenheit).

As wonderful as a constant warmth may seem (especially if you're reading this during the winter in some cold, northern state), it means there are no colorful fall leaves in autumn or white Christmases in December. There's no feel of fresh snow or smell of burning wood (unless it's a forest fire).

It also means there is no obvious springtime awaking, when trees bud and flowers come up almost overnight. If you've grown up with four seasons, they may be something you truly miss when faced with the constancy of Florida warmer weather.

Medical Care...

Have you gone to the same family doctor for years, one who took care of your kids (maybe even you when you were a kid)? What about that attentive specialist you really trust about a particular health issue? What about that dentist who made your root canal work as pleasant as possible? Not that there is a shortage of doctors and dentists in Florida, but they won't be your doctors or dentist.

It may take a while to find new doctors that are as good (for you) as your current ones. You may not even want to go through with the process of looking … especially if you or a loved one has serious medical issues.

Your Hair Stylist and Others...

Maybe it took a long time to find someone who knows how to cut your hair and they have it down to an art. You may have even followed that hairdresser when they've changed salons, even if you had to drive further to get there.

And what about other service providers? Have you gone to the same bank for 20 years? Had the same insurance agent for your home and car? Not only will you have to deal with new companies and policies, you'll also have to deal with new faces and programs. Finding people you like doing business with may be more challenging than you first expect.

Family and Friends...

Although many people who move to Florida realize they will miss the family they leave behind, they don't always realize how much they will miss them. Older couples who move here often don't know how much having their daughter or son stop by (even to just ask for a little help with something), or being able to go to their grandchild's concert, really means.

Younger couples as well, who look forward to the adventure of forging a new life one their own, often find that, after a while, they miss the nearby support and love of their parents and relatives.

And what about incredible friends? Perhaps that is your best friend since high school, or the neighboring couple you do things with regularly? What about church friends or golfing buddies or the individuals you meet for coffee a couple of times a month? Finding new people you click with might be harder than you imagine. And of course we realize some friends can never be replaced.

This may be a really important issue for children as well, especially if they're in high school. Having good friends is central to their world at that point. Moving to Florida at the wrong time could make a teen a stranger in a strange place ... and lead to isolation, depression or other serious issues.

For most people, the reality of how much they miss friends and family doesn't really hit until the holidays. Even though your children may want to come visit you in Florida for Thanksgiving or Christmas, inconvenience and expense may make frequent trips impossible.

Instead of cooking a Thanksgiving feast to share with a boisterous crowd, an older wife might find herself making sandwiches that she and her husband will sit and eat in front of the television.

Instead of going to grandma's house to have Christmas with all of the cousins, a young family may experience the loneliness of a holiday with "just them."

By itself, missing any one of the things listed above (except for family and friends) would probably not be enough to keep you from moving. But if you, or someone moving with you, would miss most everything on the list, you may want to reconsider a move to Florida (or anywhere else).

Although you might face homesickness anywhere, moving to Florida may be even more challenging because much of the population is transient. People come and go all the time. This means that even if you did find that special hairdresser or doctor you like, or finally found a neighbor you get along with, there is a possibility they won't be around for a long time.

About 1000 people leave Florida each day. This means there are more than a few Floridian neighbors, hairdressers and doctors who will be leaving eventually. So you want to be honest with yourself when asking if the sunshine, golfing or sandy beaches can make up for the friendly comforts and love left behind.

If your honest answer is "Yes" then you've mentally prepared yourself for the complete change of scenery and environment that Florida will bring. If you can't answer with an enthusiastic "Yes" at this moment, then just realize it doesn't mean you should give up on

Florida altogether. There are other options to a permanent move. We'll talk about those later in this book.

Getting Connected After Moving To Florida...

If you do ultimately decide to move to Florida then you'll want to establish new social connections as soon as possible. Thankfully, there are lots of options to do so but you'll have to pursue them.

In other words, if you embrace the mindset of making new connections as soon as possible and then availing yourself to the various avenues of doing so, then creating new social networks will help you counter many of the emotional challenges that often come with physically relocating to Florida.

So what are some of the best ways to establish an entirely new social/support network in Florida? Here are a few suggestions:

-- Churches

Churches are traditionally known for being places where one can find a community, as well as spiritual guidance. There is nothing like regular participation in a public gathering of individuals who embrace the same truths and values. But public services are only the beginning of what one can find in many churches.

There are usually regular meetings of all sorts in most churches. Scripture studies, breakfast meetings, dinners, educational functions and community outreaches - to help those in need - are generally found within the social fabric of most religious organizations.

There are many people who will attest to the reality that even though they may have attended a public worship services for a while, they never felt connected or a part of that church community until they joined at least one (or a few) of their live gatherings, meaning ones apart from the public worship services. It truly does make a difference.

-- Homeowner Associations

I am speaking here of associations that specifically cater to meeting the social needs of other homeowners in their group. For example, many retirement communities in Florida cater to those who are "55 and over."

Such groups often play a crucial part in helping those who've just moved to Florida connect with the people and resources that are a part of everyday life within the community.

-- Hobby / Special-Interest Gatherings

Some of the very best ways one might immerse themselves in new friendships can be found among others who share like-minded passions and special interests. Whether you like to sew, crochet, swim, fish, walk or mess around with boats, it's possible to find many others who share your passion in Florida. If you search out such gatherings then it's almost assured new social networks will spread out the welcome mat out … just for you. (At least it will seem that way).

-- Online Resources

The Internet has become an accepted place to find others with who have the potential to become your friends (or even family). While it's always important to never simply take an online source at face value, it's amazing how many genuine possibilities exist nowadays to connect with other real people on the net.

Websites such as MeetUp (www.meetup.com) and Yahoo Groups (https://groups.yahoo.com) and eHarmony.com are among the amazing resources that have sprung up online to help persons connect with other people. Many individuals have found such resources very helpful in getting in touch with others of like mind and interest.

There is no doubt deeply connected relationships are a part of the substance that helps create a rich and fulfilling life. If you do move to Florida, you'll probably find yourself needing them as much, or more, than you ever have in the past.

FLORIDA'S TWO SEASONS

Florida has two seasons: rainy and dry. Not surprisingly, the rainy season mainly coincides with hurricane season. It runs from June to September. In some places it rains every day, even if it's only for 10 minutes.

The other seven months are known as the dry season, where precipitation drops off dramatically. Both seasons have challenges you might want to consider when looking for a Florida home.

Floods...

In addition to the flooding caused by hurricanes is just the general flooding that can occur after a few days of rain. According to Southwest Water Management District, 41 percent of Florida is prone to flooding, and especially West Central Florida. That accounts for 14.25 million acres, many of which are heavily populated.

The rise in sea level especially presents a flooding problem in Southern coastal regions. Instead of torrential rain flowing out to sea, more of it tends to sit on low-lying land, regardless of the existence of towns and neighborhoods. Even a major city like Miami can be affected because it is currently only about six feet above sea level.

As you can imagine, the closer a home is to the water, the more the mandatory flood insurance isn't going to cost. As flooding increases, those prices will too.

Sinkholes in Florida are more of an issue nowadays too. Although they're not a new phenomenon; their frequency in residential areas in 2013 was a bit alarming. Severe flooding is believed to play a role, as is pumping for ground water, both of which we seem to be seeing more of these days.

Drought...

It's hard to imagine a place so prone to flooding during the rainy season is also prone to drought in the dry(er) season. Of the 57 inches of rain that falls in Florida on average, only 14 inches of it happens during the seven months of dry season. Between the sun, agricultural use, landscape maintenance, and human consumption, Florida's reserves in some counties dip dangerously low.

Central and northern regions in particular are affected, though southeast Florida was also hit pretty hard in 2011. These droughts affect everything from how often you can water your lawn to how much water can be used to fill your pool.

In a state that is big on reusing water, droughts can also affect the quality of the drinking water, and can make an expensive water bill even worse when a company decides to encourage conservation by raising its prices! If your house is not tied to municipal water, there is always a chance the well may run dry, leaving you with few and expensive options for potable water.

Drought also affects boating. There's nothing worse than buying waterfront property only to find there's not enough water in your outlet to get your big boat out to where you want to go. That would be a major problem if boating was a big part of the reason you moved to Florida.

Wildfires...
Just like the wet season coincides with hurricane season, the dry season also has another name. Wildfire season.

In the first four months of 2014, 686 wildfires burned more than 10,260 acres of Florida property. Many of those were in interior areas near South Florida. In the same time frame for 2013, the Florida Forest responded to more than 1,000 wildfires on 20,430 acres.

It is not only the lack of rain, but the strength of the sun that dries everything out, causing hazard conditions for wood and brush. This can be a problem in any part of the state where there are trees and brush.

If you've never been in an area with wildfire activity, it's hard to explain how unnerving the orange glow and smoke smell can be, especially when it's headed in the direction of your home.

Florida's Two Seasons

Thankfully, wildfires aren't as big of a problem as they are in California, but it is something you might want to consider before buying a house in the woods.

THE WARM WEATHER

People come from all over the world to enjoy Florida's subtropical sunshine, especially in the winter. They spend long days basking on the beach, playing golf, or touring amusement parks.

I remember my first Thanksgiving in Orlando. Instead of having a traditional dinner, we decided to take advantage of the beautiful weather and have a Thanksgiving picnic outside on the beach, something that would have never been possible back home. It was amazing (except for the seagulls). There was nothing like wearing shorts on Christmas and light jackets in January, I was enchanted with the idea of year-round warmth and sunshine.

Mine was a fairly common decision. After a pleasant winter stay, many vacationers move back to the land of perpetual sun with dreams of endless summers and mild winters. And that's exactly what they get. But it doesn't take long for others to realize that getting what they wanted wasn't at all what they had in mind.

The Sun...
Most of Florida gets between 250 and 270 mostly sunny days a year. And who doesn't love the sun? Everything is bright and happy and warm. A sunny day is like a smile from Mother

Nature. A sunny week or sunny month? Even better!

Mother Nature must be really happy here in Florida! So much sunshine means tons of time outside golfing, gardening, swimming in the pool or on the beach, and who wouldn't want to live like that?

But then summer rolls around, and for some people, Mother Nature's sunny smile begins to resemble a sadistic grin. Days get longer and hotter, and you some individuals find the relentless sunshine very unpleasant. People with dreams of year-round golf, bike rides, or walks quickly find that most summer days are too hot for outdoor activity during mid-day.

Between 13 and 14 hours every day during the summer, the sun bakes everything it comes in contact with. Concrete and asphalt become like grills. Cars can become like an oven, making any trip very unpleasant without air conditioning. Any exposed doorknob, car handle or seatbelt buckle can become a branding iron. Swimming pools often become like bathtubs. After a while, it's often more comfortable just staying indoors most of the time.

Florida heat is not only uncomfortable at times, it can be deadly. Hundreds of people every year suffer heat stroke when outdoor activity pushes their body temperatures over 104 degrees Fahrenheit. Many of these people suffer serious symptoms like seizures and unconsciousness.

Some people even die. It's not only the elderly either that get heatstroke either. Children left in hot cars, young athletes training too hard, people just out golfing, have all suffered heatstroke. We've got to be very careful about it.

The problem isn't only heat. The sunshine can be dangerous by itself. Without hats, long-sleeved shirts, glasses, or sunscreen, people working or playing in the great outdoors subject themselves UV exposure. Severe sunburn, premature aging, and cancer are just a few of such danger to the skin. Eye damage includes cataracts. UV exposure can also compromise immune systems, making it more difficult to fight off sickness and disease.

Most news stations in Florida give a daily UV report to help people know how to protect themselves in the sun. For instance, when the UV color is yellow on the news, the UV index is between 3 and 5. That means there is a moderate risk of harm from unprotected sun exposure. The report will recommend you cover up and avoid direct sun during midday.

According to the EPA, between April and August, Florida's average UV color is red, an index of between 9 and10, which means there is a very high unprotected exposure risk. The recommendation, along with covering up is, don't stay out in the sun too long, period.

The Humidity...

For most Floridians, the sun isn't what bothers them the most; the humidity is the most annoying thing about our weather. If you've never experienced high humidity on a regular basis then it's hard to explain just how it can make one feel. The best comparison I've ever heard is that of walking around in 85 degree heat with a warm, wet blanket covering your nose and mouth.

Humidity is basically the amount of water vapor in the air. It is usually measured by percentage, which is based on how much water the air can hold that day (based on the air temperature). A comfortable humidity is about 45 percent, which means the air on that day contains 45 percent water vapor. Lower humidity makes warm days more comfortable because your body can cool itself when you sweat and it evaporates.

Florida's morning humidity levels (when humidity is worst), stay in the 80s year round. This means that, very often, your sweat won't evaporate. It will cling to you and saturate your body and clothing instead. No matter how much deodorant you wear or how little clothing, you will probably spend a good deal of your outdoor time with that feeling of dampness. And without air-conditioning, humid conditions outdoors will come indoors.

Sweating is a part of the Floridian lifestyle. But be aware that humidity here also makes it a little more difficult for people with COPD issues to breathe. This may be because the air is heavier and wet air is a fertile breeding ground for allergens and mites, which aggravate respiratory afflictions, including conditions such as asthma and emphysema.

Mold also flourishes in high humidity and heat. Towels, bathing suits or cloth lawn furniture can become dotted with inky spots when left out too long, sometimes within a matter of days. Inside the house, mold can grow more easily here in Florida. Mold can cause different respiratory problems, especially in those who have allergic reactions.

The good news is almost every place in Florida is air-conditioned. Most residents go from their air conditioned homes, to their air-conditioned cars, to their air conditioned offices, to the air conditioned stores, and then back to their air-conditioned homes again. And they do this with relatively little exposure to the regular heat and humidity.

We Floridians minimize the effects of the sun, heat, and humidity just by staying indoors much of the time, although electric bills will remind us of what we're doing. But it's a part of our lifestyle and we just accept it. It's just important for anyone that wants to move here to realize that staying indoors in order to avoid the warmer weather and temperatures is the common routine for most residents here in the Sunshine State.

ABOUT THOSE HURRICANES

For those of you dreaming of that home on the sandy shores of Miami or some other coastal town, there is something you need to know. From the beginning of June until the end of November, Florida passes through hurricane season.

What does that mean for you beach lovers? It means that, along with enjoying the gorgeous sunsets and sandy beaches in summer, you'll be the first to meet any hurricanes or flooding that may pass nearby during these months.

Not that there are major hurricanes in Florida every year, but when they hit, they can be dangerous (and expensive). Between 2000 and 2013, Florida experienced 63 hurricanes. Those storms were responsible, directly or indirectly, for 150 deaths and more than $60 billion in damage. In 2004, a particularly active hurricane season, one out of every five homes was damaged in some way.

Hurricane season is cited as one of the main reasons people who move to Florida decide to leave, especially after a bad storm season. They say the stress is just too much. So it is something to take into consideration.

A Little about Hurricanes...

Hurricanes begin to form as ocean waters warm. The water evaporates from the ocean's surface, condenses into rain and clouds, and low pressure causes spiraling winds, which form the storm's eye. These storms can begin in either the Atlantic Ocean or, less often, the Gulf of Mexico, which makes either of Florida's coasts, the Keys, and its southern tip, particularly susceptible.

At first, these storms are called tropical cyclones, but they are upgraded to hurricane status when wind speeds hit 74 miles per hour. At that point, a hurricane is considered a category 1. A category 5 is the highest rating and accounts for any hurricane with winds above 157 miles per hour. Hurricane Andrew, which hit Southeast Florida in 1992, had winds up to 177 miles per hour. Historically, the worst month of hurricane season is September.

What You Can Expect...

Hurricane season brings a host of issues apart from the actual storm that you might want to consider before plunking down a ton of money to live somewhere on a Floridian coast.

Coverage Ad Nauseam...

If you're a news watcher, be prepared for constant coverage on all things hurricane. For six months (and especially at the beginning of the season) you may be exposed to "how-to-pack-a-hurricane-kit" news segments, hurricane anniversary stories, what-to-do-if-you-need-to-evacuate tips and the like.

As actual storms form and slowly move, you will be kept up to date with radar and sometimes hourly progress for days. If a threat moves from watch to warning, you can expect hurricane news to be the focal point of every local station.

Not the worst thing, because you should be informed, but the constant coverage may become annoying. A constant diet of hurricane news adds to daily stress for many people, and it may engender unreasonable fear.

Storm Surges and Flooding...

Hurricanes often bring storm surges, which are extreme increases in water levels along the coast. The force of hurricane winds can drive water levels 11 or more feet above average levels. As you can imagine, such a surge could cause terrible damage - even wash away vehicles and houses. And unlike hurricanes, there is really no way to adequately protect against them.

Most neighborhoods in Miami are at an average of six feet above sea level, while South Daytona's average is 6.5. Cocoa Beach, also on the East Coast, is a little higher at 12 feet. But as you can imagine, all of these places are highly vulnerable flood areas.

Heavy rain and surges can quickly turn low lying areas into flash flooding, unpassable roads and soaked yards. Plus, it brings a host of other problems. Flooding is definitely an issue in many other areas of Florida too.

Winds...

If you've never lived in a high wind area, even pre-hurricane winds can be scary. Not only can wind damage to homes and trees, it can turn objects like lawn chairs, plant pots, and tree limbs into projectiles.

Such objects need to be securing during periods of high wind to keep them from crashing through windows and such. Hurricanes can also spawn tornadoes at times, which move faster than their host hurricanes and cause even more damage.

Blackouts...

High winds invariably cause downed trees and power lines, which means no electricity. Hurricane Wilma (in 2005), left more than three million people without power for at least eight days ... and some people for more than two weeks.

No lights, television, or computers can be a problem, especially if you work from home. More of a problem is the lack of refrigeration, and corner stores run out of water and ice quickly.

Apart from that, the thing most Floridians miss during electricity blackouts is air conditioning. This is especially the case during the middle of the summer. No air conditioning may be a serious problem for older folks and young children, as they may have a lower tolerance for heat.

Evacuations...

Probably one of the most difficult parts of hurricane season is the evacuations that may take place in coastal areas. How often do they happen? It depends.

Some seasons are pretty mild. In 2004 and 2005, however, Florida experienced eight major hurricanes, which caused evacuations for many thousands of residents. Although evacuations may occur as far inland as Orlando, it doesn't happen very often. It is the Florida Keys, or coasts, that are more likely to be evacuated.

When local government authorities decide a hurricane is a real threat, they will issue a mandatory evacuation a day or so ahead of time. Now, this doesn't mean local deputies are going to come drag individuals out of their homes and force them to leave. But it does mean that, if one chooses to stay in their home, local emergency services are under no obligation to help should help be needed. In other words, those residents are on their own.

Evacuations are no fun. In addition to getting your home ready for the storm (we'll cover this in a minute), you'll have to find a place to stay. And so will everyone else being evacuated. Hotels at a safe distance fill up quickly. You may have to find a hotel further away than you had originally planned on going. That could be a frustrating process.

You'd also have to decide what to take with you. There are the obvious items, like clothing and toiletries, but then there are the things that — should a hurricane damage the home — you want to be kept safe. Important documents, jewelry, and photo albums all need to be gathered or safely stored quickly so you can get moving.

Gas also sometimes becomes an issue as local residents scramble to fill up car tanks and generators. Lines at gas stations can get long, and some people get cranky.

Then there's the actual leaving. If you get going behind others, you may be subjected to long traffic lines at a crawl-and-stall pace. After an hour or so, you may decide to turn off the car air conditioner to conserve gas, which will only serve to make the trip less comfortable.

Along the way, you're bound to see a few unfortunate souls on the side of the road (or even in the middle), who have already run out of gas. And there will likely be the occasional honking and hollering that seem to accompany such experiences too.

The thing to remember about evacuations is that, in themselves, they are no indication that a hurricane is going to definitely hit the evacuation area. Since the hurricanes of '04 and '05, officials seem much more likely to call for evacuations than they were in previous years.

Hurricanes are temperamental, and often change course. So what eventually comes may be little more than a glorified thunderstorm passing overhead. An evacuation for that sort of thing leaves many people feeling as if they've wasted time, energy, expense and effort … for nothing.

What You Can Do…

If your desire to live in Florida outweighs potential inconveniences (or downright dangers) that accompany hurricane season, then there are some things you can do. After all, you always want to minimize any possibility of damage to your person, family, home, and finances.

Doing all the right things is obviously no guarantee one will ever escape all hurricane seasons unscathed. But taking sound precautions will improve their chances tremendously. As Edna Mode, from the animated movie, The Incredibles, put it, "Luck favors the prepared."

Before Moving…

Even though you've always wanted to live in a condo on Miami Beach, you make look at some other options that might be less susceptible to hurricane weather. Mid and Northern Florida have their own charms and are still within driving distance to many beaches. The chances of one's home being severely damaged by a hurricane in Orlando are far less than in Key West.

If you decide you have to be close to the beach, consider a stilt house or a house constructed after 2005. Just also be aware that homeowners in "high risk" areas pay much higher insurance rates and may also be required to purchase additional flood insurance.

Considering a home in more inland areas may help you avoid storm surges. The highest elevation in Florida is still only 120 feet above sea level though. Flooding from heavy rains may still be a problem wherever one goes in Florida.

When looking for a home, try to avoid high risk flood zones (online sources and realtors can help you) and consider carrying flood insurance even if you aren't required. Also look for a newer home, constructed after 2005. The building codes for these houses were modified after the large hurricanes of prior years.

Houses built after 2005 are supposedly better able to withstand floods and winds. Be sure to find out whether your house is equipped with hurricane doors and impact-resistant windows. These will offer added protection for your home, inside and out.

After Moving…

Once you have a home in Florida, put together a hurricane kit. The size and contents will vary according to your family's needs, but here is a basic list to use for reference (be sure to have everything packed in a tote or other waterproof container):

- Basic toiletries
- Batteries

- Battery-powered radio
- Bug spray
- Canned foods (don't forget the can opener!)
- Cash
- Dried foods
- First Aid Kit
- Flashlight
- Manual charger for cell phone
- Matches
- Paper products
- Sunscreen
- Trash Bags
- Water (stored in glass if possible)
- Water purification tablets

After your kit is assembled, take some time to think through an evacuation plan. Include a list of needed tasks, names and phone numbers of possible places to stay, and a list of important items to bring (include your hurricane kit and vital documents).

If you live in what is considered a "high-risk" area your county will already have an evacuation route mapped out for your zone. Be familiar with it.

You might also think about having an "evacuation fund" … some money that will defray the cost of extra gas, a hotel stay, and possibly even missed work time. The website www.ready.gov also has some tools to help residents organize their own evacuation plan. Having a well-thought out plan in place before potential storm events can do wonders for stress levels during any real evacuation.

Another thing to consider is the possibility of buying a portable generator, with ample supply of gas. Generators can offer a power alternative if a hurricane takes out electricity for a prolonged period of time.

If your budget allows, you can actually have a full back-up generator system installed in the house, which can run everything, including the air conditioner, if the electrical grid goes out.

Evacuation...
When a mandatory evacuation is called, reference your evacuation plan. One key is moving quickly. You might even assess a particular situation and deciding to evacuate prior to an official mandatory evacuation. Even if you leave town early, only to have a hurricane later change course, consider it a drill that will help better prepare you in the future.

Get gas as soon as you can. Getting to gas stations early could save you from a long wait. While you're doing that, perhaps have your spouse or older child begin making temporary living arrangements.

If you already have the phone numbers of targeted hotels (or friends/relatives homes) then this will make the job easier. I cannot stress how important it is to get things done as quickly as possible. Those who move early and fast will be the ones who obtain gas and places to stay with less hassle.

Before leaving for an evacuation, you'll want to secure your house. This means shuttering windows (or putting up plywood) for older homes, putting patio furniture and yard toys in the garage, and locking everything up tight. But this also means securing pets. If a pet needs to go with you, be sure the hotel (or home of your friend or relative) will allow it.

Ideally, you'll want to get onto your planned evacuation route as soon as possible. A full-scale evacuation would mean many thousands of other people moving out of the area the same time as you. That means every second counts.

Some people prefer waiting until the last possible moment to evacuate. By that time everybody else has left and there is the possibility of less traffic. The chances of downed power lines and less visibility (when driving) are the risk. You would want to avoid being in a hurricane while driving on the road.

Other people prefer not to evacuate and just ride most storms out at home. If you ever decide to do that then be sure your house is buckled tight and the hurricane kit is ready if case you need it.

ABOUT FLORIDIAN BEACHES

Florida has been one of the fastest growing states for decades. Since the '80s, the population has doubled, and the 2013 census estimated the population at more than 19.5 million (not counting snowbirds, which are about 1 million). Florida now has the fourth largest state population, and is less than 100,000 people behind the state with third largest: New York. That's a lot of people.

In a lot of ways, the population growth is fantastic. Growth brings more money, more businesses, and more jobs. The once laid-back vacation state is now filled with booming industries, and busy cities. Progress, it's called.

But there's always a price to pay for progress. In Florida, that price is the very thing so many people move here for: the beach life. The abundance of places to relax, swim, and fish are indirectly being diminished by the amount of people coming to enjoy it.

Everyone who has been to a little Florida beach town falls in love with simple bungalows, pristine shoreline, clear water and interesting little shops owned by interesting people. But all that's changing at an alarming rate.

More and more of these little towns are beset upon by more traffic, bigger roads, luxury houses, and franchise businesses. Empty landscape is quickly snatched up and transformed into huge hotels, subdivisions, or parking lots. Old buildings are knocked down to make room for newer ones, all to accommodate the growing amount of people who want to live by the beach.

Many beaches, meanwhile, become less and less attractive. Instead of solitary walks on sandy shores, visits to the beach become an afternoon of dodging Frisbees and sunbathers.

Not only that, beach parking fees are getting higher, beach parking lots are getting bigger (at the expense of the beaches!), and the sand and water become littered with trash. Add this to the beach erosion brought about by natural causes and man-made dams and jetties, it's hard to tell just how long Florida will be known as the land of beautiful beaches.

It's not only the shores that are suffering. The water itself is becoming polluted, even dangerous at times. The multitude of hotels, golf courses, and luxury homes require massive amounts of chemicals to keep their lawns looking beautiful.

That's all well and good until storm season, when the torrential downpours wash all the toxic weed killers, fertilizers, and pesticides out of the lawns and into the waterways. Apart from the potential damage to drinking water and seafood, these chemicals are believed to be a factor in a far worse problem -- Florida red tide.

Red Tide...

Although it is not a new problem, its frequency and intensity seems to be increasing. Florida red tide is a high concentration of certain toxic algae that kills fish and causes respiratory distress in some humans and pets. Although it is safe to swim in (some people may get a rash), the thought may not be too appealing when you see all the dead fish floating in the current or lying on the beach.

Red tide also affects waterways and can make fishing and trapping seafood tricky. This is because some seafood, including clams and mussels, absorb the toxins. This can make people sick after eating them. Between the smell of rotting fish and the irritation of toxins to lungs and skin, red tide — which can last for months — can make any beach experience unpleasant.

Beach Closings and Warnings...

There's nothing like going to a favorite beach only to find it closed. It's something that happens more frequently these days, especially where the water is monitored regularly.

In 2013, some counties closed certain beaches for 10 or more days. Three beaches in Monroe County were closed for more than 20 days each and three in Gulf County were closed for more than 30 days. One of the biggest contaminants is a bacterium known as fecal coliform which comes from — you guessed it — feces. A lot of beaches don't close, but it could be because they don't test the water quality on a regular basis. What we know won't hurt us?

All this is to say that if your dream of moving to Florida revolves around sunny days at the ocean be sure to do your homework about your desired destination's beach conditions before you move. This is easy to do online. Just find Florida forums and post questions. Locals who aren't trying to make a commission will tell you like it is … unlike many realtors, who often try to make the beaches still seem like the paradises new residents want them to be.

CREATURES GREAT AND SMALL

It is true. Florida is one of the most beautiful states in the country. Its sub-tropic climate is conducive to an abundance of flora and fauna, making it a paradise of fruits, flowers and trees.

But along with being a garden of paradise, Florida is a haven for critters of all sorts ... from creepy crawlers clear on up to potential predators. And although not all of these creatures are exclusive to Florida, the frequency with which they can be found may be.

Let's start with the bugs. This part might be an unpleasant shock for some who have only been to Florida's resort areas and never been bothered by a bug. That's because resorts use copious amounts of pesticides, thus not representing a true view of the Florida pest situation.

One source has identified 244 different kinds of bugs in Florida. Of these, a few of them are most loathed by newcomers and old-timers alike. Those are palmetto bugs, fire ants, Florida love bugs, and wolf spiders.

Palmetto Bugs...
On a visit to Florida, this was the first bug I saw. There were a bunch of them teeming around the bottom of a tree in the front yard. I got closer

to look. They were brown and oblong and about two inches in length. They looked like huge cockroaches.

When I asked about them, I was told they were palmetto bugs (named after a plant) and not to worry, they didn't like to come in the house. Just then, one just took off flying, and almost ran into me. Now, I'm not afraid of bugs, but these creepy crawlers were nasty. Needless to say, I avoided that part of the yard for the rest of my stay.

Don't let the name fool you. Palmetto bugs are nothing more than giant flying cockroaches.

Fire Ants...

On the night I was leaving on that same trip to Florida, I met another species of bothersome bug. This time I never saw him (or them as it were) coming. Before we got into the car, I put my bag down in the grass on the front lawn so I could give my relatives one last round of hugs.

When I finished, I put my bag in the back seat where I was sitting. Then we all got in the car and drove away.

We couldn't have gone more than a mile before I began to feel a burning sensation on my behind and legs, and it kept spreading! We pulled the car over and once we turned the overhead light on, I caught my first glimpse of fire ants.

They were tiny little red things with a mean bite. Evidently I had put some part of my bag on or by their nest and they didn't like it. Luckily, there were only about 20 or so in the car and we were able to kill them, but the bites stung for hours! When I later moved to Florida, the first thing I learned to do was avoid their nests, which look like little more than a low-lying pile of sandy dirt.

Florida Lovebugs...

Thankfully these little creatures don't bite. But they do pose a hazard, namely to your vehicle. During their mating seasons which happen around the end of April and the end of August, these bugs (often in mated pairs) fly around Florida in thick swarms.

If you happen to drive into any of these swarms, the front of your car or motorcycle will be plastered with their little gooey bodies. Because they're acidic, their body chemistry can ruin your paint job if they're left to bake on. In extreme case, they can even affect the performance of your car by clogging the airflow through your vehicle's front grill.

Wolf Spiders...

These big —and I mean big —spiders are completely harmless to humans, but can very intimidating. These hairy creatures can grow as large as two inches, about the width of someone's palm. If you can stand to have them around (outside the house, of course), wolf spiders can actually help keep other spider populations down.

Mosquitos and Termites...

Although you have most likely dealt with both of these critters in whatever state you are from, you may find yourself dealing with them on a much larger scale in Florida where the warmer, moister climate provides supreme breading conditions.

Mosquitos are most active in the early morning and at dusk and, depending where you live, can be really bad. Add that to the more recent arrival of gallinippers— a mosquito that is 20 times the size of an average mosquito — in Florida and you may find these pests an annoying deterrent to any outdoor activity.

Sometimes towns will spray insecticides to keep mosquito (and other bug) populations down, but in some areas you will be left to fend for yourself. Ingesting vitamin B (1 and 6), apple cider vinegar, and garlic helps some people, while others find dryer sheets (in pockets), or bug spray are the best way to stop from being bit.

Termites are a particular threat to homeowners. Yearly check-ups around your home will keep them from destroying one of your most valuable assets.

Along with bugs, there are other, more dangerous creatures in Florida you should also be aware of, as you may come in contact with them while out exploring, out on a jog, or even on the beach.

Snakes...

There are about 45 native snake species, most of which are in North Florida. Six of these snakes are venomous, including three types of rattlesnake, copperhead, cottonmouth (water snake), and coral snake. Although snakes try to avoid humans, because of residential expansion, they occasionally end up in the same spaces, especially in parks and on trails.

Another snake worth mentioning is the Burmese python. Although it is not native to South Florida, it certainly has established itself there with growing populations.

Most of these snakes live in the everglades, and mostly pose a threat to Florida's other wildlife like deer and bobcats. They have become so numerous that in January of 2013, the Florida Fish and Wildlife Commission had a contest to see who could hunt down the most pythons. The contest included cash prizes for the longest and the most.

They have also become more invasive in the last year or two. In 2013, a man riding around with his friends in Florida City spotted a python on the side of the road and decided to capture it. What ensued was a ten minute battle, with the man finally cutting the snake's head off to free himself from its deadly grip. That python turned out to be the longest one on record in Florida — a whopping 18 feet and 8 inches. The same year a ten foot python crawled into the yard of a Miami resident and strangled their 60 pound Siberian husky.

Alligators...

Unlike the Burmese pythons, alligators are native and can be found in all parts of Florida. They prefer fresh water lakes, slow-moving rivers, and wetlands, but can also be found in brackish water. Official estimates vary but it's believed that between 1.3 and 1.5 million gators call the Sunshine State their home.

With all of these alligators, there are only about a dozen reported attacks a year -- with no deaths since 2007. But with a ratio of approximately one alligator per every fifteen Floridians, the chances of spotting one are pretty high.

The thing with alligators is they may show up where you least expect them. You might discover them in lakes or canals where you planned to fish, boat, or swim. That will probably result in a change of plans.

Another popular place for gators is, believe it or not, golf courses. This is because so many courses have been built by wetlands and ponds. In general, however, alligators do their best to avoid humans and most humans are smart enough to do the same.

One of the first things you'll learn about alligators when you come to Florida is not to feed them. The last thing anyone wants is Floridian alligators associating humans with food.

A word of caution: even though alligators avoid humans, they have no problem snatching up dogs that get in the water, so don't let your dog's swim in a lake or canal where alligators have been spotted (your neighbors will know). Don't even let them close to an alligator. The huge reptiles are deceptively fast and would make a fast meal of your pet while you stand by helplessly.

Sharks...

In April of 2014, a shark fisherman on the Northwest coast of Florida caught a huge Mako shark from land. It was 11 feet long and weighed more than 800 pounds. Thankfully, those are not the kind of sharks most Floridians need to be concerned with.

During the spring, thousands of sharks migrate around the coast of Florida. Mainly these are blacktips and spinners under six feet long, and on their way somewhere else. But for whatever reason, in the past few years, they have been coming closer to shore, mainly posing a threat to beach goers, swimmers, and boogie boarders.

In spite of all the millions of people who enjoyed Florida beaches in 2013, only 23 were attacked, and none of those attacks were fatal. And though they are attacks to us, they are merely cases of mistaken identity to the sharks, which are just looking for dinner. If anything, the sharks can be more of an annoyance because shark sightings cause entire beach closings.

FLORIDA BOOMS AND BUSTS

When the economy is good in Florida, it's very good. Businesses are booming, homes of all kinds spring up in large numbers and jobs are plentiful. But when the economy turns bad, well, it's a bust.

Businesses seem to dry up and blow away. Jobs become much harder to find. People leave, often selling their houses for half of what they paid for them just a couple of years before. These are just a few of the things that are particularly noticeable when a recession kicks in here.

Although most states see their share of economical flux, Florida's ups and downs seem to happen faster and also seem to be a little more extreme on either end of the scale, whether good or bad. Knowing this can help you buy, sell, and do business at the right time.

There was a time when the cost of living was generally considered to be very inexpensive in Florida. It was one of the reasons people retired here. A couple could sell their house wherever they lived, and buy more house in Florida for less money. Because food and commodities were also less expensive than in other states, a retired couple's hard-earned savings would last longer.

Such is no longer the case. According to statistics based on research from the Council for Community and Economic Research, Florida is 28 on the list of states with the most affordable cost of living. This isn't terrible, but it certainly isn't what it was even 10 years ago.

A big part of the current economic problem was the bottom falling out of the housing market and the global recession, which officially started in December of 2007. Not only did Florida lead the country in foreclosures, much of its lucrative housing industry dried up when the rate of people moving to Florida slowed from 400,000 people a year to 100,000 people a year.

Thousands of construction workers and people in related fields were left unemployed. When people aren't working, they aren't spending money at restaurants and local businesses. Those businesses, in turn, start hurting.

There are other volatile variables that make Florida subject to more extreme economy cycles. Because tourism is such a huge part of Florida's service economy, any downturn in visitors per year also translate to lost jobs, closed businesses, and less revenue for the state as a whole. After the beginning of the Great Recession, tourism slowed considerably, which only added to the troubles Florida was having.

In addition, agriculture is a huge part of Florida's economy, especially oranges. Sixty-seven percent of oranges sold in the United States come from Florida. Florida oranges are used to make 40 percent of the world's orange juice. Vegetables are a major part of the huge agricultural industry here, and according to Florida's state site, it leads the southeast in farm income. But in 2004, hurricanes alone did 2.2 billion dollars' worth of damage to crops. Between the two deadly seasons of 2004 and 2005, Florida lost 17% of its citrus groves -- and 12,000 jobs along with it.

The overall unemployment rate was still as high as 11.3 in 2010, one of the highest rates in the nation. The housing market was still struggling. It was actually a good time for retirees and skilled workers to buy a home.

Although Florida has lagged behind the rest of the country in recovering from the 2007 recession, things are starting to look a little brighter. Starting in 2011 tourism levels began to rise. In 2013, tourism hit record-breaking levels of 89.3 million people visiting from all over the world, which is fantastic for service industry workers and business owners. The influx of people moving to Florida has also started to increase again, which means an increase in housing costs and construction jobs. These events have helped decrease the state's unemployment rate.

One thing that workers need to know is that full-time work with benefits can be hard to come by in Florida. Competition for well-paying jobs with benefits can be tough.

For healthcare workers, one positive thing about Florida's proportionately larger senior population is there seems to be an abundance of healthcare jobs available at every level. Actually, any job that caters to the senior population is usually a safer bet, regardless of Florida's economy cycle. When housing picks up, construction jobs are also widely available. And skilled workers serving the tourism industry are always needed.

If you are still working and are highly skilled in a particular area, not only might you have more trouble finding full-time work, you may not be happy with the pay once you do find a job. Chances are you will not make the same kind of money you did in the state you are originally from.

The balance is the lower cost of living. Young couples, however, may want to think about moving to a part of Florida that has jobs available in their field. This should definitely be of higher priority than moving close to the beach or to a town they love. Remember, you can't eat pretty.

Although the job market may be a bit dismal at times, owning a business will be a different animal. If you have enough knowledge and skills to start a service business in an area where the population is exploding, you can earn a good living.

Before the housing crash, boatloads of construction companies were making small fortunes because there was so much business.

Additionally, places like restaurants, barbers, gas stations, mechanic shops, and health food stores all become incredibly lucrative because an influx of new people are looking for services. If you're business is the only choice in a new area, you're the one who gets the business.

Businesses that cater to seniors are, as I mentioned before, a fairly safe bet. Medical supplies, services, and products that make senior living easier are always going to be in high demand in the retirement capital of the country. Just be sure to pick a product or service that isn't already oversaturated or over-served.

Of course the obvious factor here, especially in Florida, is that good times don't last always. As quickly as business opportunities, prices, and markets go up is often as quickly as they can come down. Hurricanes, floods, and other unexpected factors can have a big impact on all of Florida's major economies, making it particularly susceptible to major swings. But if you know this and plan accordingly it will help you stay prepared by not overextending yourself financially or panicking when the price of your house falls or your business slows down.

If you're willing to stick it out through the ups and downs, then you'll be okay in the long run. But if a fairly stable state economy is important to your fiscal and mental health, then Florida may not be the place for you.

Florida Booms and Busts

Florida is in an upswing of its economic cycle, which makes it a better time to buy and do business here (at the time of the writing of this book) than it was just a couple years ago. How long this growing economic climate will continue is hard to tell. Being forewarned about Florida's economic ups and downs may help you decide if you're willing to risk taking a ride on its roller coaster if you're not retired.

DIFFERENT APPROACHES
TO LIVING IN FLORIDA

One key to being happy after moving to Florida is figuring out how much of the year you actually want to be here. You can go all in as a full-time resident. But there are many part-time living options available. Only you can decide which avenue is best for you.

Living in Florida on a part-time basis is often the best choice for many individuals. Let's discuss part-time residency first.

Living in Florida Part-Time...
Some of the happiest people who live in Florida much of the year are those who come as "snowbirds" or "halfbacks." These folks might live in Florida up to six months a year and in some other state the rest of the time.

These residents are often northerners who follow warm weather. The come to Florida in the winter and live in their originating state during the summer.

In a sense, they enjoy the best of both worlds. They enjoy nice weather and holidays with family and friends, maintaining, to some degree, the life and culture they have always known. Then, when the weather turns cold, and they're ready for some time away, they settle down in Florida for a spell and enjoy all it has to offer.

The great thing about being a part-time Floridian is the choice of living options available. We'll look at four of them.

Rent...

As you can imagine, seasonal rentals (also known as turnkeys) are a very popular option. These are fully-furnished, all-bills-included, condos or homes that rent on a month-to-month basis.

For the person or family looking for an extended winter vacation of one or two months, this is a very good option. Not only can a seasonal home be rented for the cost of a week or two at a resort, everything one needs is already there.

Things like dishes, cookware, washer / dryer and even linens are included. This option allows you to really "live" in Florida - enjoy the pool, walk to the beach, cook out - part-time, without all the hassle and expense of owning two properties.

Own in Two Places...

If you find that a short winter reprieve of one to two months isn't enough, then you might want to look into owning two homes. If you want to stay between three months and half a year it may be best for you to own a Florida residence, in addition to your present home. Of course, this assumes you can afford to maintain the cost of owning two homes.

A second home in Florida will provide you with an escape from both cold winters (up north) and humid, hurricane-prone summers (in Florida). This plan works especially well for retired people who want to both hold onto their northern ties and own a piece of the Sunshine State as well.

Owning in two states is not difficult. Some retirees keep their original home, while others downsize and then sell a big home up north and then buy two smaller homes -- one in each location.

Because most Florida winters generally don't entail a lot of heating or air-conditioning costs, one can generally keep household temperatures at minimum levels. It may even be possible for homeowners to pay utility bills in both residences for the same cost they were paying year-round in a bigger home. When housing prices are down in Florida, two smaller houses becomes an especially reasonable option.

Once you own a home in Florida, if you are willing to register your car, change your driver's license, and a few other things, you can then claim Florida as your primary residence. This means you can take advantage of Florida's tax breaks and asset protection. Truly, this is probably the best option for people who have worked hard their whole lives and want to enjoy the financial advantages of both worlds.

Be Stationary and Mobile...

For the more adventurous among us, another viable option is owning a home in one state and owning a motor home you can drive to another state. For instance, you could keep your home in a northern state and travel south to Florida after the holidays ... or when the birds start to leave in the Fall. You can travel at your own pace, enjoy scenery and meet new friends along the journey.

Once you get to Florida, there are hundreds of places to park all over the state. And you can choose your scenery too. There is everything from rustic national forest to ritzy RV resorts.

Like hotel rooms, RV spots have different rates, depending on the type of park and the length of time you plan to stay. Sites also have different levels of service, from basic water and electricity to cable television and Wi-Fi. If you find a spot in Florida that you really like, you may even be able to book it at the same time next year. Such an arrangement would make that special place a semi-permanent landing spot on your migration.

Another advantage to mobility is that once you've had your fill of Florida (most likely when the heat and humidity start kicking in), you can head back north. You can then park your "other" home right alongside your main residence ... just in time for the nice weather.

Another option might be the reverse: owning in Florida and traveling to your original home state during the summer and fall. You may not find many resort areas, but most states have ample campgrounds. You also might be able to just park in a relative's driveway for your stay, especially if you have your own generator. As a Florida resident, this approach may allow you to own "more home for less money" in Florida, while also having the asset protection afforded to its full-time residents.

Of course the RV option isn't for everyone. But if you've always dreamed of traveling and seeing the country, buying an RV and owning in one place, or another, would be another way to try and enjoy the best of both worlds.

All-In Floridian...
At this point in the book, if you still want to move to Florida full-time, let me suggest something. It may seem like a lot of trouble, but, in the long run, it could save you and your family tons of time, money and stress.

My suggestion is this: before you sell your house, pack all your belongings, and head south, do a trial run first. What I mean is, before making a final decision, live in Florida for at least six months -- in the summer.

I know this may seem extreme, but I can't tell you how many people who move to Florida and end up moving out again in a year or two, at a great expense. Imagine the costs associated with selling your home, moving your belongings, buying a new home, and fully establishing yourself in a new place.

What would it cost when you add up realtor fees, moving expenses, inspection and deed fees, and closing costs? The cost is easily in the thousands, perhaps even tens of thousands. Then imagine doubling costs because, after a year or two, you realize you hate living in Florida.

You might hate being so far from home. You might hate the insurances costs. You might hate the weather most of the year. And that's not even counting the lost equity in a house if you happen to leave at a time when housing prices are down.

Many homebuyers who moved to Florida in 2007 and then moved back out in 2009 lost as much as 65 percent of the equity they had in their home. I don't know anyone who would knowingly choose to lose that kind of money and experience that kind of emotional distress, especially in their golden years.

This is why I suggest a trial. A trial run will give you some time to keep one foot planted where you are and use the other foot to test the Florida waters. And vacations don't count either! Try six months to nine months of off-season, daily grind, before completely deciding to dive in.

One good thing is that because Florida has so much seasonal housing it's relatively easy and inexpensive to find places to rent in the off season (April through December). There are all kinds of seasonal living options in most parts of Florida. This means you'll be able to find something close to where you were thinking about buying.

A trial run can also help you decide if you really want to live on a waterfront, in a small house, or in a condo. Again, because these homes are already furnished, you can save on moving costs by just bringing what you need for the time being.

An off-season trial will give you a much bigger picture and understanding of what living in Florida really is all about. You can experience its economy first-hand and compare the overall cost-of-living to what your expenses currently are at home. You can get a taste of the politics, acquire an awareness of crime rates, and experience the true culture of the area you think you want to move into.

Living in Florida full-time is much different than coming here on vacation. You will be subjected to the humidity, the bugs, and perhaps even occasional loneliness.

Facing such issues on a daily basis may make you realize that you were better off where you were, or that you're definitely more snowbird material (as opposed to full-time resident). At that point, you can move forward with more confidence and considerably less stress then if you discover these realities after making an expensive, hard-to-change move.

WHEN BUYING REAL ESTATE IN FLORIDA

So you've decided to move to Florida and want to own your own home in the Sunshine State. Here are some hints to help you make a choice that best suits your needs.

Decide What and Where...

You may already have the "where" is mind. It is most likely someplace you've already vacationed, such as the Keys, Miami, Daytona, Sarasota, Naples or Orlando.

No matter where you decide, if you're stuck on the idea of living in or near a certain city, let me encourage you to be a little open-minded. There are many small towns close to these bigger cities that may be more suitable, more affordable, and less crowded (especially in the winter). Increase your chances of finding the right house by enlarging your home search area to include a couple of close-by towns.

You may also have already decided on what kind of a home you want to own. Your choice will mainly be between a condominium and a single family home. You can find either of those, in various settings ... in a community, in the country, or on a waterfront.

Condominiums are a popular choice -- at least at first -- for snowbirds and half-timers. They often offer benefits such as community living, fabulous swimming pools, gorgeous golf courses, and meticulously kept grounds. Plus, these types of amenities are billed as convenient and maintenance-free.

If you enjoy taking care of your own yard and don't like living quite so close to neighbors, or if you have young children around, single family homes are a serious option. Having your own space gives you more privacy, makes it easier to spend time outside, and makes it easier when family come to visit. Single family homes come in all shapes and sizes, and can be found in a variety of settings, as can condominiums. The most popular homes in Florida currently feature three-bedrooms, two-baths and a two-car garage.

Let me say a little bit about choosing a home by a waterfront. If your reason for wanting to live on a canal is because you plan to buy a boat, try to find a real estate agent who specializes in waterfront property. They will be able to tell you about the ins and outs of water levels, docking, and the pros and cons of boat owning in any particular area.

After thinking it through, you might realize that owning a boat and living on the waterfront isn't as important as you first thought. Much of what you pay for this type of home is for water access. You may decide your money would be better invested more inland, where you can get more house for the same money. You are also less likely to be flooded, which is always a consideration for properties next to waterways.

The same is true for beachfront property. Are you really willing to pay a large amount of money for an occasional morning walk on the beach… or for the view? You might be, and if that's the case, just be sure to buy a house that has stilts or some other type of elevated foundation. If, upon further consideration, it turns out living right on the beach isn't as important as you first thought, it might be worth looking into what that same money will get you just a few blocks down the street.

Another option when considering a single family home is whether or not you want a pool. This too is strictly a matter of personal preference, but is something one should think about very carefully. It will be much easier and cost-effective to buy a home with an in ground pool already installed than to add one later on. The same is true of in ground spas.

Many newer homes have caged pools -- a pool enclosed in a screen house of sorts, which is definitely a plus. Not only will the screened enclosure help keep leaves and debris out of the pool, it will also keep most mosquitos (except for the tiny ones) and other bugs from ruining your pool time. The cage also keeps other things out, such as unsupervised children, frogs, snakes, and the occasional alligator that might be passing by your property.

Start Small...

Chances are that the house you're leaving behind is a decent size. It could be the home you raised your children in, or a house that's been in your family for a couple of generations. You are most likely used to plenty of space to move around in and to use for storage. You also might have had a huge yard and lots of property for kids to run around on, to have your garden, or to host a fourth of July picnic.

When you move to Florida, you might want to think a little differently. For most people, moving to Florida is an opportunity to downsize (and for good reasons). They no longer need as much space for children, or for things, or for used heavy blankets and snow gear.

Many people in Florida spend as much time as possible outdoors. I've seen many Floridians use their porch or covered driveway as another room (an outdoor extension of their home's interior), complete with couch, television set, and grill. On nights when the humidity is bearable, these people will come outside, have friends over, play cards, and cook into the wee hours of the morning.

Many newer Florida homes may not have a huge amount of inside space. But they'll often sport generous screened outdoor spaces (known as lanais) that allow people to walk out of their back door and into a bug and critter free zone that may or may not include a pool. These lanais are a perfect place to set up an outdoor living and dining room area and many people do.

With these things in mind, a retired couple moving from a 3,000 square foot home in another state will often be quite content in something with less than 1,500 square feet of space in Florida. Although so little area may not seem like a lot, floor plan options that offer cathedral ceilings, open areas between rooms, and screened in places for outdoor living usually prove to be more than ample room. Such floor plans are also more affordable for many homebuyers.

Shopping…

Once you decide on what size space you want, where, and for how much, ask your realtor to make a list of homes that fit the criteria. Then have the realtor show them to you, starting with the least expensive. Try to take as many notes and pictures as possible so you can remember what you like and dislike about every house.

Once you find a size/layout/price that is attractive, focus on seeing more houses that are in that range. You're more likely to find the right home using this approach.

Be careful about letting a realtor talk you into looking at bigger or more expensive homes if you are fine with something smaller and less expensive. Being firm and decided will help you from being overwhelmed by all of the possible options during the shopping process ... and subsequently remorseful after you buy.

Newer May Be Better...

It's worth mentioning again that flood policies can add a small fortune to mortgage payments. Because older homes do not adhere to newer flood codes, the payments based upon the price paid for an older home may seem like a good deal, but you could be paying a whole lot more for flood insurance afterwards.

Find out the numbers for the house you're interested in. Carefully do the math. For instance, you may find an older home with payments about $1,100 a month. That may sound like a great deal until you find out it's in a high risk flood zone, and because the house is older, flood insurance is going to add an extra $500 a month to the expenses. By doing research, you may find out that the mortgage, plus flood insurance cost ($1600), is the same for a larger, newer house. Not only could you pay the same for a better product, a newer house construction (they are elevated above the road), lessens the chance of you actually having to deal with floodwaters in a domicile.

Read the Small Print...

Here is another frequently given word of advice among Florida realtors. Before deciding to move into a condominium, gated community, or subdivision, find out what rules, regulations, and restrictions you will be subject to after signing the lease. Even if you love the particular property, you may find it won't be worth dealing with a long laundry list of rules. There are few things more annoying than militant homeowners' associations and tattle-tale neighbors.

In a condominium, you will most likely have very little to say about anything that happens outside of your front door. You may or may not be allowed to have anything on your front porch (including decorative items or plants). And you probably won't be able to set up a hammock in the backyard. You will also be liable for ongoing maintenance fees to pay for the landscaping and pool. And you may not be able to have much say in how the money you pay each month for those things is administered.

Condominiums have a disclosure of such conditions and restrictions (rules and regulations), and by law, have to give them to you when you sign an offer on such a property. But these documents can be nearly 100 pages long at times. They are often hard to follow too. It will be in your best interest, however, to read every bit of that disclosure and rules document.

If you get the disclosure and are appalled at being told whether or not you can have a pet or use a grill, how many people you can bring to the pool, or what you're allowed to wear in the common areas, you are given three days or fifteen days (if working directly with a condominium developer) to rescind your offer and back out of the deal. This is why it's important to read these documents. Once you sign the contract and your time is up, you are obliged to keep those rules until you sell the property. Not keeping the rules of condo associations can result in hefty fines, liens, and having to defend yourself in small claims courts.

Another important thing to be aware of is that there is no grace period to back out of a deal if buying into a deed restricted community. That will often be the case if you move into a gated community or even some subdivisions. Deed restrictions are rules on how you must maintain your house and yard, what you are allowed to do and not do in the neighborhood, and what can happen if you don't abide by the rules.

The purpose of these restrictions is to keep property values up for everyone, can be a good thing, if that is important to you. Most people would agree they don't want to live next to someone who has six old cars in their yard and a washing machine on the porch. But some of the rules may be petty, like how long you can keep your garage door opened, how long your grass can grow, or whether or not you can install a pink flamingo ornament in your yard. They may also dictate house colors, roof material, and rules pertaining to lawn furniture.

Do yourself a favor and be sure to ask your real estate agent about deed restrictions on any house you are interested in. Be wary of signing anything until you full read about any property's restrictions.

Deed restrictions are often policed by a Homeowners' Association (HOA) -- a group made up of volunteer and vested neighbors. Your real estate agent might not even inform you that they exist. But the next thing you know, your HOA may be requiring hundreds of dollars in yearly dues and telling you what you can and cannot do on your property.

Unfortunately, HOAs have a pretty bad reputation in Florida. Up until last year HOAs didn't really have to answer to specific authorities within Florida. However, in July of 2013, the State passed a law requiring HOAs to register with them. Whether or not that will have any direct impact upon how such associations operate is yet to be seen. At the time of this writing HOAs can still make a lot of trouble for residents if they feel those residents aren't following the deed restrictions to the letter.

If you're a "rules person" by nature and have no problem abiding by HOA restrictions then you may be very comfortable living in a deed restricted community, or a condo, for that matter. But if you're not a "by the book" person, like expressing your individuality, and like having your yard and the outside of your house the way you want, then steer clear of rules and regulation controlled properties. Buying a home in a deed restricted area may not provide you with the peaceful Florida existence you've been dreaming about.

Be in It for the Long Haul...

As I mentioned previously, Florida's housing market can be pretty volatile. Home values can fluctuate dramatically, even within just a couple years. Depending on where Florida's economic cycle is when buying real estate, the value of a house could double in less than five years. It could also drop by half in the same time frame. The downturn in value could be terrifying (or financially crippling) if one decides they want to leave Florida in the middle of a recession or real estate downturn.

If you move to Florida with your eyes wide-open to the good, bad, and the ugly, however, then your chances of getting caught in such a situation are minimized. If you come here with a good idea of whether you're a full-timer, halfback or snowbird, and if you aggressively look for the home that is perfect for you; then you'll put yourself in a much better position for success. You'll be able to sit back and enjoy your new home without too much regard for its value in five or ten years. Making a quality and informed decision about moving to Florida can save you the hassle of having to making choices such as whether or not you should sell at a bad time, or staying somewhere you don't want to be, or renting to tenants who most likely will not take care of your house like you would.

If you decide to stay in Florida long-term then you'll have an advantage over those less educated. You now know that rising and falling real estate prices often play a huge part in Florida's cyclical economy. If you ever decide to sell your home in Florida then you want that decision to be on your terms. It's always better to sell at a time when home prices are up.

For some, moving to Florida fulfills their dream. For others, a few precautions, mixed in with topics we've talked about in this book, may have spared them lots of expense. May you make the right choice for you.

ABOUT HOMEOWNER INSURANCE

If you find your Florida dream home, do yourself a big favor and find out how much it's going to cost to insure before buying it. You may find out the price of insurance is more — much more — than you want to pay. The last thing you want is to get stuck with unreasonable insurance rates that continue to climb, even in good years when there are very few hurricanes or floods.

Homeowners Insurance...

Insurance is quickly becoming one of the reasons people rethink their original intention to buy a home in Florida. According to the National Association of Insurance Commissioners (NAIC), Florida has the most expensive home owner's insurance in the country, with an average premium of $1,933. That is twice as expensive as the national average. And those numbers are from data for 2011. Prices have increased since then.

It wasn't always that way. In 2003, an average home might cost the homeowner $500 a year. But after the brutal hurricanes of 2004 and 2005, insurance companies had to pay out 3.5 billion dollars in claims, something they don't like to do. Many smaller insurance companies went belly-up. Bigger insurance companies sometimes refused to even sell insurance in Florida. This resulted in the State taking steps to offer Citizens Insurance to keep people from losing their homes to foreclosure.

Many big insurance companies like State Farm, Liberty, and Farmers still operate in Florida, but on a limited basis. This means you might no longer be able to get coverage with a company you've been with for years. Newer policies probably won't be as good either, at least for the same price you're paying now.

The Florida Office of Insurance regulation offers a real-time tool that shows average insurance rates for different insurance companies in different counties. Let's look at average insurance rates (with wind mitigation) for a home built before 2001 and valued at $150,000.

In Leon County, home of the state's capital Tallahassee, 2014 average rates are estimated between $863 (with Florida Peninsula) to $2031(Liberty Mutual). Prices for Marion Country, where Orlando is located (with the same two companies) range from $1013 to $2638. Palm Beach county rates were between $2713 (Florida Family) and $9,500 (United Property and Casualty). In Miami-Dade County, rates ranged from $4383 (First Protective) to a whopping $13,264 (United Property and Casualty).

These prices are for policies with a two percent hurricane deductible, which means homeowners are going to have to pay substantial amounts of money out of pocket before any insurance coverage begins covering storm damage.

Eye-opening, isn't it? And here's the kicker. These policies do not cover flooding. In many areas of the state, it is mandatory that homeowners buy additional flood insurance.

Flood Insurance...
In January of 2014, a Florida news source featured an article about a couple hit with a $24,000 flood insurance bill for their new vacation home in Miami. They had no other option than to pay it or lose their new home. A homeowner in Saint Pete's Beach recently saw his flood insurance go from $1,900 to $7,400 in a single year ... and that's after raising his deductible and dropping insurance on the contents in his home.

Although prices aren't that high for all homes, legislation passed in 2012 did allow for flood insurance rates to increase for the National Flood Insurance Program policies, especially for older, low-elevation homes. The rate increases affected 270,000 Florida homeowners.

Although NFIP is currently the only option for the vast majority of mandated flood insurance in certain areas, recent legislation has tried to encourage wider participation from new and currently funded flood insurance providers.

You Can't Always Get Insurance...

In addition to sometimes paying through the nose, you can't just get insurance anytime you want it. In some counties, if you happen to be unlucky enough to try and close on a house when a named storm is brewing, you may not be able to buy insurance until the danger of the storm has passed. This law was enacted to keep homeowners from insuring when their house was in danger and cancelling when the danger had passed.

An unintended consequence however is the expense, headaches, and hassles for newcomers who find themselves holed up in hotels and storing their furniture until they can get insurance and close on their new house. If a newcomer procures insurance but hasn't finalized the sale before a hurricane passes through, the insurance company can refuse to honor their commitment until a representative comes out to check for damage.

This could take a while if the hurricane has damaged other properties because all the representatives will be busy handling current customers. So this can hold things up for newcomers even if their home wasn't damaged.

Thankfully, the past few years have been relatively quiet, hurricane-wise. But it's always wise to assume hurricanes and floods are a constant threat to home ownership in Florida. They are always a very real factor when it comes to Florida housing. Insurance prices will continue reflecting the possible cost of damages that can occur from hurricanes. You may think twice about whether you're willing to foot these yearly bills.

FLORIDA TAX SAVINGS

With all the financial challenges you will be taking on if you move to Florida, there are a few positives that will make your financial life easier, especially if you're a homeowner. Florida is considered to be one of the better states to live in terms of tax savings.

State Income Tax...
Florida is one of seven states that have no state income tax. In other words, you will not pay taxes on income of any kind — including interest and dividends — to the state of Florida.

This is true even if you live in two states. If Florida is considered your principle residence, then you don't have to pay any state income tax. Not only do you get to keep more of your money, you have one less form to send in every year, which is a timesaver.

Homestead Exemption...
Even though some people pay a small fortune for their home insurance, taxes on that home should be less burdensome. This is because the first $50,000 of assessed value is not taxed. The explanation for this is that not taxing the first $50,000 of property values helps offset the estimated values of homes that may quickly rise

during periods of real estate booms ... especially ones when lots of people move to Florida.

In Florida, real estate taxes are paid at the end of the year, but the application for exemption must be submitted by the first of March. The home you are applying the homestead exemption for must be your primary residence.

It can't be a vacation home, and it can't be a home you rent out, unless the home is multi-family, as in duplex or triplex. In that case, you can apply for the Homestead exemption as long as you, the owner, live in one part of the home.

If you're over the age of 65, an additional $50,000 exemption may be available if you are at a certain income level (that number changes, but your county assessor will know). There are also other exemptions for qualified widow(er)s, military personnel, and people with disabilities, so it is definitely worth checking into.

Before you apply, though, you'll have to have all of your other "Florida ducks" in a row. In addition to producing a deed and owner(s) social security numbers, the county assessor will want copies of your driver's license and vehicle registrations -- all from Florida -- and all with the address of the property you're applying for.

Sliding Property Assessment...

One of the greatest things about owning real estate in Florida is the way property value assessment is addressed when it comes to property taxes. Each county does property value assessments every year, and, like in most states, when the value of a property goes up, the property taxes go up. But unlike many other states, if your property is devalued for some reason, your Florida county will (imagine this) lower your taxes. This a great help, especially in Florida's housing market, which can swing from feast to famine in a relatively short time frame.

FLORIDA ASSET PROTECTION LAWS

In addition to the great tax benefits you would get as a resident of Florida, you might want to consider the very favorable asset protection afforded to Floridians. It is one of the best states in the entire country for protection of home equity, retirement funds, and annuities.

Accidents and financial misfortune can happen to anybody, but Florida's asset protection can also be particularly important for small business owners who, for whatever reason, might be sued. Of course, I'm no CPA or attorney, so you definitely want to check the ins and outs of this information with professionals before taking action on it.

In most other states, being sued for accidents or by creditors can easily destroy life savings. Bankruptcy or lawsuits could more easily cost residents their homes and life savings. But this is not the case in Florida.

Just being a permanent resident allows some hard-earned assets to be protected. This might give you peace of mind about your finances in a way you may not have if living somewhere else in the country.

Asset Protection for Your Home...

What if you have a $500,000 home on a small lot in a Floridian municipality and you get way behind on your credit card bills and the credit card company sues? Or what if you are in a terrible car accident and are sued?

If you own less than a half-acre in a town or city, or less than 160 rural acres, nothing on that land can be touched by creditors, regardless of how much it is worth. In Florida you cannot be ordered to sell your home to pay off that debt.

Your home is considered off-limits to creditors, regardless of the amount of equity you have in it. It's worth mentioning that this home equity protection also extends to declaring bankruptcy. In most cases, however, the amount of time one has lived in Florida may affect the situation.

Asset Protection for Retirement Funds...

Wouldn't it be awful if you were sued for something, and if the judge ruled against you, you were made to forfeit all the hard-earned money you had been saving for many years? That can happen in most states. You could be ordered to liquidate anything and everything you had saved for retirement in accumulated retirement funds in order to pay off the judgment.

But once you're a Florida resident, and you move your IRA, 401k, or other retirement savings, to a Florida financial institution, your savings are automatically protected from being seized to pay off any judgments. Of course, this may not work if you live somewhere else and are sued before moving to Florida. But long-term residents can rest assured that no such misfortune is going to destroy their retirement savings accounts when they'll need them.

Life Insurance and Annuities...

Two other assets protected from financial misfortune are life insurance policies and annuities. For a policy owner, any cash value of, or proceeds from, a whole life insurance policy cannot be seized to pay creditors. The same is true of annuity payments. Once again, such personal values and income are protected automatically if you become a Florida resident.

This kind of automatic asset protection is something you will not find in most other states and. Next to the sunshine and beaches, it's definitely an important part of the financial benefits associated with moving to Florida.

FLORIDA'S 7 REGIONS

The remaining part of this book covers Florida's 7 regional areas. The following chapters offer an overview of these regions, which collectively make up the territory in the State of Florida. Every region offers both residents and tourists a bundle of unique characteristics and defining features.

Each chapter provides a brief summary of the climate and history of the particular area. But there is also a lot of relevant information with regards to 2 types of residents: those associated with young families and those considering a move here as retirees. With this in mind, we're going to talk about the main cities and towns many Floridians consider to be the "best places to live" in these various portions of our lovely State.

This section of the book gives you a significant amount of information that cannot simply be "googled" or otherwise found on the Internet easily. Depending upon what you're looking for in the way of both personal goals and needs, you may, at some point, save a great deal of time and money with it. I hope you use the information in the following pages as a basis for planning when it comes to visiting and/or moving here.

Florida's 7 regions include:
1) Panhandle/Northwest area

Florida's 7 Regions

    2) Northeast/Jacksonville area
    3) Central West/Tampa area
    4) Central East/Orlando area
    5) Southwest/Naples area
    6) Southeast/Miami area
    7) Southern Florida Keys

Now let's have a look at each one...

THE PANHANDLE

The remaining part of this book covers Florida's 7 regional areas. The following chapters offer an overview of these regions, which collectively make up the territory in the State of Florida. Every region offers both residents and tourists a bundle of unique characteristics and defining features.

Tucked far in the western corner of Florida, sits an area known as the Florida Panhandle. Residents refer to it as Lower Georgia as its terrain and temperatures are more similar to Georgia than the rest of Florida.

Approximately 100 miles in length and with an average of 75 miles width, this region consists of ten counties plotted to the east of the Apalachicola River. Apalachicola is a quaint city that is actually known as the "Oyster Capital of the World."

Slower and less tropical that Southern Florida, the Panhandle still has a plethora of offerings for its residents. The larger and better known cites are Tallahassee, Pensacola, and Panama City.

TALLAHASSEE
The Florida State capital is home to the 2014 NCAA Football National Champions of Florida State University. It is also home to Florida A&M University, as well as several junior colleges and the Aveda training school. This is a college town

that can run the gauntlet from packed weekend traffic to cricket quiet during university holidays and breaks. With a college town comes massive amounts of young people and a host of bars and clubs.

Climate

There is no ocean breeze to cool down the sultry summer days where the temperatures can easily exceed 100°. The fall is gorgeous with bountiful and colorful leaves cascading to the ground. It has actually snowed in Tallahassee before, and do not be surprised to get a few tornado warnings in the spring. You will, unlike much of the rest of Florida, experience all four seasons in the state capital.

History

Tallahassee has a strong and active Seminole history. The tribe is still quite active with FSU and actually designs the costumes and regalia for Chief Osceola and his horse Renegade, the FSU mascot. It was once a British and a Spanish colony. The city became a city and the capital in 1821.

Outdoor and Fun Entertainment Offerings

Tallahassee has many family friendly events and festivals. Some of the best for families are the:
- First Friday at Railroad Square
- Parks and Greenways
- Wakulla Springs
- FSU Rez
- Greek Food Festival
- Doak Stadium
- Cascade Park complete with amphitheater

On Sundays, take a leisurely stroll around Lake Ella with your dog or visit the perimeter shops and cafes.

Best Place for Young Families and Retirees to Live

The east side of town is a bit more family and retiree friendly. Less college students live there. Two of the best sections are Killearn and Buck Lake.

Job Market

The biggest employers for the city of Tallahassee are Florida State University and the Capital. Currently close to 62,000 people work for the university. There is an active hospitality market, but keep in mind the tips and pay in the food and hotel sector will be lower in a college town. Jobs in other fields could be scarce to find.

Average Cost of Living
- Consumer Price Index: 84.85
- Rent Index: 23.89
- Groceries Index: 102.64
- Restaurants Index: 71.95
- Consumer Price Plus Rent Index: 55.55

The cost of living index is based on a 1-120 point scale. The higher the number, the higher the cost. The consumer price index is the average of all the other statistics such as rent and grocery. An example would be London, which hits the scale at 118.

Places to Stay Away From

Any inner city that is active should be avoided late at night and early in the morning. Tallahassee is no different. Places to avoid would be south of the capitol and some of the areas north of the campus.

PENSACOLA

Pensacola sits on the piece of the Florida coast known as the Emerald Coast. The waters are crystal clear and the pace is slow, except during Spring Break. This beach on the Big Bend of Florida is a popular destination for college Spring Breakers, so from March to May expect bikinis, heavy traffic, and a rowdy group.

Climate

The coastal breeze is lovely and the climates are warmer year round than in Tallahassee. The mercury never dips below forty or soars below the high eighties. This bend bound city is quite prone to hurricane hits. Eight hurricanes have made entry in Pensacola:

Eloise (1975) ... Frederic (1979) ... Juan (1985) ... Erin (1985) ... Erin (1995) ... Opal (1995) ... Georges (2004) ... Ivan (2004) ... Dennis (2005)

History

In Pensacola's 450 plus years, it has been under five different flags. The Spanish, French, British, Confederate, and US flag have all flown over the city.

The Spanish liked the city so much they had three different periods of rule there.

Prior to this, the first recorded history was documented in 1686, as the Native American tribe the Pensacola, after which the city was named, lived in the area.

Outdoor and Fun Entertainment Offerings

Fish from the Pensacola Pier, sun and fun at the beaches, or dive the sunken ship The USS Oriskany, a scuttled aircraft sunk in 2006, which is now the world's largest artificial reef.

The Downtown area has a viable art population. There are art museums, local music festivals, and it is the locale for the Vietnam Veteran's Wall of the South.

Best Place for Young Families and Retirees to Live

Gulf Breeze is an excellent place for a family to settle. There are quite a few parks and the schools are consistently rated high. For retirees, the beach area has some condominiums that have active programs and outings for retirees. CNN recently rated it as one of the 25 best places for retirees to locate. Since 1958, the company Veranda has played a strong role in Pensacola retirement communities.

Job Market

Pensacola is home to two large companies: Monsanto and Westinghouse. Monsanto has been in the area since 1953 and Westinghouse employees over 4500 people. The fishing charter business thrives in the area. In the Escambia River alone there are over 85 different species of fish. The military has a large presence in the area with the Corry Station Naval Technical Training Center and the Naval Hospital.

Average Cost of Living:
- Consumer Price Index: N/V
- Rent Index: 31.38
- Groceries Index: 86.66
- Restaurants Index: 73.67
- Consumer Price Plus Rent Index: N/V

Places to Stay Away From

There is not a true big city feel here, so Downtown is completely safe and is going through a robust revitalization phase. After the last few hurricanes, some buildings sat empty for a while causing a brief surge of crime, but right now the area as a whole is quite safe. My advice would be to find other activities to experience than the beach in the spring.

PANAMA CITY

Panama City is a bit similar to Pensacola, but much smaller. Sitting on the corner of the Gulf of Mexico and Andrews Bay, it is a popular family tourist location. Residents like the laid back and affordable beach side living the hamlet offers. However, the Spring Break crowd is massive and at times, seemingly out of control.

Climate

This mild climate rarely dips below 60° or climbs over 90°. The last hurricane to hit was Earl in 1998. Beware the humidity in the subtropical city. It can get intense and a ponytail may be lady's best friend. The range is 52% to a whooping 93%. The closer to 100% humidity means the more water in the air saturation. 93% is soggy. It does have a short late summer rainy season.

History
Like much of Florida, Panama City is steeped deep in the history of Native Americans. The Spanish named the city in the 1500s, as they explored the rich fishing area. Pirates liked the fact that the many juts and pockets in the coastline made for perfect hiding places. During the Civil War, a small aquatic skirmish occurred just off the current Panama City Beach location. The modern city, as we know it, debuted in 1936 under he guidance of developer, Gideon Thomas.

Outdoor and Fun Entertainment Offerings
In addition to the beach, there are oodles of family activities. There is mini golf, arcades, festivals, a great Halloween Haunted House, and Pirates, yes pirates! The Sea Dragon is a replica pirate sea adventure excursion. The city is proud of its over 200 acres of city parks and the city has an active children's sporting league that runs year round with different sports offerings.

Best Place for Young Families and Retirees to Live
Most families tend to be situated a bit west of the coastal area in West Bay and South Port area. The homes have more square footage, the yards

are bigger, here are more parks, and the schools, such as West Bay Elementary, have excellent reputations.

The average house cost in Panama City is $ 120,000.00. So combine that cost with the large oceanside retirement community offerings and the city becomes a magnetic draw for retirement plans. The city is small averaging about 38,000 people.

Job Market

As with typical coastal cities, the tourist industry is large. The biggest employers are:
- Tyndall Air Force Base
- Bay District Schools
- Bay Medical Center
- Wal-Mart
- Naval Support Jobs

Average Cost of Living:
- Consumer Price Index: 57.92
- Rent Index: 38.69
- Groceries Index: 62.70
- Restaurants Index: 51.26
- Consumer Price Plus Rent Index: 48.68
- Local Purchasing Power: 37.87

Places to Stay Away From

The crime rates soar in the beach areas during the spring. Most crimes reported are property theft related. When at the beach while the spring crowd is a presence, be aware of your possessions and the crowd around you.

APALACHICOLA

Apalachicola sits at the point where the Apalachicola Bay and the Apalachicola River meet. The harbor village looks as if it should be in New England. Most of the homes are sprawling Victorians or quaint cottages. The whole of the town, with its 2300 year round residents, is overlooking the bay.

The city has a historic designation, so there are not chain stores. There is not even a supermarket, only a local general store. The town is proud of its 900 certified historic homes.

The annual Seafood Festival in November would be great family excursion. Arts, craft, and yummy treats are for sale, and the city will crown Miss Florida Seafood! Apalachicola is also proud to boast that it supplies 90% of Florida with its oysters and 10% of the nation with its oysters.

This city is of off the beaten path, so if you thrive on cars, beeping horns, and the cosmopolitan life, this is not the place for you. The schools get an above average rating and the entire city is perfect for young families and retirees who do not require the bustling city life amenities.

NORTHEAST REGION

If you long to live in a Florida coastal big city, but still want the niceties and courtesies of a small town, then you should be house hunting in the Northeast sector of Florida.

Daytona Beach and Jacksonville offer bustling city life and kinder and gentler people. These Florida cities are more affordable that their hot-blooded city cousins down south. Amelia Island is smaller city in the northeast region of Florida, but quite the hidden gem that offers numerous fun for the family.

JACKSONVILLE

As you drive over the I-95 bridges hovering over the city, you can look down and see the massive town with the St. John's River weaving past it. This Duval County city is the largest population and land sized city in the state of Florida. Over 1,400,000 people reside in its 747.0 square mile perimeter.

The city has professional sports' teams, is home to the Wounded Warrior Association, and is the site for one of the best private schools in the nation, Bolles. The Riverwalk area is bustling with young executives and just to the east, the wide beaches welcome you to dip in the Atlantic waters.

Climate

Jacksonville has remained unscathed by hurricanes for the last 12 years when Hurricane Fay dropped by for a visit. In 2012 Tropical Storm Beryl skirted the region. Meteorologists attribute the low hurricane hit rate in Jacksonville to be the way the city is tucked into the Florida coastline.

The temperatures are mild and there is a slight winter season. The mean temperatures run from 50° to 85°. If relocating to Jacksonville, go ahead and sell your winter coat.

There are some very low-lying areas that are prone to flooding. Your home may not be eligible for flood insurance if it sits in one of these spots. Check this carefully before signing on the dotted line.

History

Shards of pottery found in the Jacksonville date back to 2500 B.C. The area, like much of Florida, has a rich Native American history with the Timucua tribe. Jacksonville has suffered two large disasters with the fire in 1901 that wiped out most of the existing town, and the devastating 1964 Hurricane Dora. The city is in the midst of an economically sound boom and regrowth.

Outdoor and Fun Entertainment Offerings

The Riverwalk has many shops and restaurants. During the day it is perfect for family outings, but as the sun begins to dip, the crowd size increases and becomes a a bit more boisterous.

Jacksonville is home to two US Navy bases. If you have never watched a ship come in from duty, you must take the family to do. This entire experience is heartwarming.

Jacksonville is home to the Jaguars (football), Barracudas (ice hockey), Suns (minor league baseball), and JAM (ABA basketball). You just have to decide which game to go to because at any given time, three-four could be playing.

Jacksonville Beach is wide and not as congested as other Florida beaches. The family would enjoy fishing, boating, or swimming. As of late, there has not been a large Spring Break presence.

Best Place for Young Families and Retirees to Live

Home prices vary drastically in Jacksonville. If you are looking in the half million to over a million range for your family, consider the neighborhoods of Pablo Creek Reserve, Glen Kernan, or Queen's Harbor. If that is too rich for your blood, James Place and Deerwood are in the $ 250,000-300,000 range. All of these neighborhoods have parks, pools, and a family feel.

Jacksonville has a numerous amount of retirement communities. The most desirable ones are Emeritus at Mandarin and Cathedral Residence. All of them have an activity schedule and program that will keep you hopping.

Job Market

The job opportunities are rich and varied in the area. The US Navy, various sports' teams, Baptist Hospital, and the local school system have a constant need for new employees. As with any coastal town, the hospitality industry is hiring around the clock.

Average Cost of Living:
- Consumer Price Index: 76.98
- Rent Index: 37.82
- Groceries Index: 83.65
- Restaurants Index: 66.11
- Consumer Price Plus Rent Index: 58.66

The rent index, groceries index, restaurant index, and consumer price plus rent index are averaged to come up with a consumer price index score. The score is based out of 120 (the higher the number the higher the cost). Sydney, Australia has a mean score of 118; whereas Jacksonville's mean score is 76.98.

Places to Stay Away From

As with any large city that is split by a major interstate, there are some pockets of crime. Play it safe and stay away from north of I-10 and west of I-95. Also, any area north of 20th Street and south of the Trout River can be sketchy(the northwest area of Jacksonville).

DAYTONA BEACH

Daytona Beach, home of NASCAR and those wide beaches you can drive a car on, is in the Florida northeast region. It is south of Jacksonville, and to the east of I-95. NASCAR comes to town twice a year, and the traffic virtually comes to a standstill (except on the actual race track). Daytona Beach also plays host to Bike Week.

Climate

Obviously as you move further south, the temperatures are going to become more tropical. The temperatures range from 50° to 90°. The Daytona rainy season is in the month of July, expect thundershowers to roll in almost very late afternoon.

History

Just like Jacksonville, this city was a Timucuan post. Additionally, the Seminole and the Creek Tribes also had a sizeable population in the area. The British and the Spanish both flew flags of possession over Daytona. The city proper was formed by a purchase of sizeable acreage by Mathias Day. He built a hotel on the area where historic Daytona sits today.

Outdoor and Fun Entertainment Offerings

Beyond the NASCAR events and the beach offerings, there are many activities for a family to enjoy in Daytona Beach. The city has quite a few parks and a sports' league for kids. Their site www.fun4daytonakids.com will help you keep all the offerings straight.

The Art League of Daytona Beach offers classes as well as presents exhibits. Additionally, the Museum of Arts & Sciences is a family favorite.

Best Place for Young Families and Retirees to Live

The market is in a bit of a slump in Daytona; the areas near Clyde Morris and Beville are quite nice and affordable. In both places, children can walk to school.

The AARP has named Daytona as an affordable place to retire. The median house price is around $ 115,000.00 and the retirement community has settled into quite a few of the beachfront condominiums like Plaza Resort and Ocean Garden. A nice two-bedroom beach rental can be had for around $1000.00 a month.

Job Market

Two of the biggest Daytona employers, bedsides the hospitality industry, are NASCAR and Raydon Corporation, a technology company. Thousands of people work for NASCAR, and at any given moment there are dozens of job listing for the racing industry in Daytona.

Average Costs of Living:
- Consumer Price Index: 79.98
- Rent Index: 37.82
- Groceries Index: 83.65
- Restaurants Index: 66.11
- Consumer Price Plus Rent Index: 58.16

Transportation has helped the city grow and prosper. The arrival of the railroad by Flagler and then the onset of the racing world both played roles in making Daytona Beach what it is today.

Places to Stay Away From

While the beach is very, very slowly experiencing a slight resurgence in economics and construction, there are some spots near the beach where abandoned buildings and structures are in disrepair. Also beware of the strip of land just off to the west of the interstate.

The crime rate spikes during the February and July NASCAR races, as well as during Bike Week, in the spring, so be vigilant during that time.

AMELIA ISLAND

Amelia Island is a quaint village bound to the west by the Intracoastal waterways and to the east the Atlantic Ocean. Main Street has cute shops, cafes, and seafood restaurants. The streets are wide and the porches on the historic homes are even wider.

There are dozens of bed and breakfasts, which is one of the larger job markets in the town. You can ride a horse along the sugar sand beach, golf at one of the many courses, tour Fort Clinch, or try your luck on one of the numerous chartered fishing boats.

Amelia Island proper is an excellent place to raise a family. Think evening strolls down to get ice cream cones. The schools are good and while the cost of buying a home can be costly, just off the island the prices drop considerably. A three bedroom home on one of the 50 historic blocks will cost you at least half of a million.

The Ritz Carlton on the beach is another one of the city's biggest employers. There are also hospitality and fishing industry employment opportunities. Located near the beach is a popular retirement community called Osprey Village.

CENTRAL WEST REGION

Tampa is known for its bay and tarpon and the entire west central Florida area is dotted with ports, coves, keys, islands, and inlets. While Tampa and Clearwater may be the most well-known destinations in this region, also consider historic Sarasota for your new home.

The west central Florida plot is less fast-paced than its east side counterpart, but it is also less expensive. The rugged and jagged coastline holds many hamlets, small towns, and coastal potentials, as well as the metropolitan Tampa for you to consider as your Floridian home.

TAMPA

Tampa is the nation's 54th largest city, but it has a warm and welcoming vibe like a small town. The golden onion shaped domes of the University of Tampa and the massive Bay Bridge are two very recognizable iconic landmarks. The Bob Graham Sunshine Skyway Bridge is well known for being struck by a ship in 1980. The Travel Channel considers the bridge to be one of the Top 10 Bridges in the World.

The city is located in Hillsborough County and is Florida's third largest city. There are 208 private and public schools combined, and it proudly sits on Newsweek's List of Best High Schools. Make sure to stop by Bern's Steak house after hunting for your new abode, it is internationally known and each and every bite is a culinary delight.

Climate

A hurricane came knocking on the door of Tampa in 2004, but relatively speaking the area has had very few hits. The local emergency page states that Tampa has less than 1% chance of a direct hit.

In the summer, there will be scattered afternoon showers. Floridians call these sun showers. They are usually short in duration and you can be back at the beach or on the tennis courts before you know it!

History

Did you know that in 1513 Ponce de Leon arrived in Tampa? He was still searching for the Fountain of Youth. The Spaniards were not impressed with the west central area and instead moved east. The first real development of the region came in 1824 with the construction of Fort Brooke.

Outdoor and Fun Entertainment Offerings

Tampa is well known for it fishing fare, especially the multitude of tarpon. Other fun besides fishing could take place at a Buccaneers game, Lowry Park Zoo, the Florida Aquarium, the IMAX Theater, Busch Gardens, or one of the many art museums in the area.

Check out two of the local and quite viable children's sport leagues called i9 Sports or the P.A.L., Police Athletic League. You can also visit the Carrollwood Cultural Center for camps and clubs concerning the arts. Tampa also offers creepy but fun ghost tours that take participants through the city's historic district exploring haunts.

Best Place for Young Families and Retirees to Live

If your family prefers an upscale and historic neighborhood, then check out Hyde Park. It is close to downtown and surrounded by parks and green spaces. Safety Harbor is a lovely family friendly neighborhood with bike paths, a local library, and it is close to a fishing pier. Espiruitu Catholic School is located in Safety Harbor and has been nationally recognized for academic excellence.

There are nineteen active age 55+ communities in the area. Some of the favorites with the most offerings are Kings Point, Timber Pines, and the Tampa Bay Golf Community that boasts a 27-hole golf course.

Job Market

Amazingly, over 55 companies in the area employ over 1000 people. Tampa is headquarters for Publix, Raymond James Financials, and Tech Data. The Tampa Bay Buccaneers are a big source of employment and the tourist and hospitality industry, such as Busch Gardens, always have openings. The job market is robust.

Average Cost of Living:
- Consumer Price Index: 76.97
- Rent Index: 37.84

Central West Region
- Groceries Index: 83.66
- Restaurants Index: 66.12
- Consumer Price Plus Rent Index: 58.16

The rent index, groceries index, restaurant index, and consumer price plus rent index are averaged to come up with a consumer price index score. The score is based out of 120. (The higher the number the higher the cost).

The railroad debuted under the guidance of Henry B. Plant in 1884, but the port was where the money and action lay. It is now the seventh largest port in the United States with a flourishing cruise and phosphate shipping industry.

Places to Stay Away From

As with any large city, the crime rate will be higher downtown and near the interstate. The only region as an entirety that may be dangerous would be Temple Terrace. There seems to be a consistently higher crime rate there. It has a 29.07 per every 100 people rate for violent and property crimes per year.

CLEARWATER BEACH

Clearwater is 26 miles of barrier islands. You can watch the dolphins roll by and go crabbing for fun. The movie, Dolphin Tale, the true-life tale of Winter, Clearwater Marine Aquarium's tailless dolphin, has people strongly considering Clearwater as a relocation possibility. It is the quintessential small town Florida beach destination.

Many of the businesses are locally owned which instills a sense of ownership and community. The Palm Pavilion Beachside Grill & Bar has had a mere two owners since opening in 1926 as a burger joint, bathhouse and Skeet-Ball joint. It is a lovely city for you to hang you hat.

Climate

The average temperatures run from 50° to 90°. July is the warmest month and January is the coolest month. The rainy season falls in the month of August. In the past 150 years, only three hurricanes have made landfall in Clearwater. Traditionalists attribute this to a Native American blessing, but the fact is the placement of Clearwater requires a sharp hook by a hurricane for entry into the city.

History

The Tocobaga Tribe settled Clearwater. Fort Harrison was constructed in 1885 and used as a supply outpost during the Seminole War. In 1489 people were offered 160 acres if they were willing to cultivate and protect the land. During the Civil War, the city fought for the Confederate side.

Outdoor and Fun Entertainment Offerings

The Start Smart program, a nationally recognized children's soccer program, is based in Clearwater. The Clearwater Marine Aquarium is great for a day of fun and it offers summer camp and kids' programs. Boating, fishing, and water activities are always a good time. The Clearwater Parks and Recreation Division has an Aging Well Center, an adult baseball league, parks, as well as a dog park. Activities abound for Clearwater denizens.

Best Place for Young Families and Retirees to Live

Clearwater is just north of Tampa, and many people who work in Tampa, but want a cost friendly city, live in Clearwater. High-end family friendly neighborhoods are Island Estates and Harbor Oaks.

There are 18 advertised retirement communities in Clearwater. Horizon Bay is close to shopping and dining, and has a full activity schedule. And Regency Oaks has thrived for the last 30 year because it also features an assisted living component.

Job Market

The top local businesses that are always hiring are Tropicana Inc., with 3200 positions in total; Onyx North America an environmental service company; and Boars Head Provisions.

Average Cost of Living:
- Consumer Price Index: N/V
- Rent Index: 36.49
- Groceries Index: 98.67
- Restaurants Index: 76.88
- Consumer Price Plus Rent Index: N/V

Places to Stay Away From

Out of a 100 ranking (with 100 being the worst), the Clearwater area rates an 11 on the crime index. The chances of becoming a victim in Clearwater are one out of 150 people. The area north of downtown and the sector east of downtown to US 19 should be avoided if possible.

SARASOTA

In a recent Gallup-Healthways survey, Sarasota ranked 23 out of 189 places (1 would be the most desirable) for living satisfaction. The quaint and quiet historic town is a lovely place to raise children or to retire.

There is a Riverwalk area with shops and restaurants, a designated historic area with museums and cultural offerings, and numerous amounts of family friendly parks and public areas.

The city has 71 certified historical structures. Florida's designated state art museum is in Sarasota, The John and Mabel Ringling Museums of Art. There is an Education, Library, and Conservation Complex as well as a miniature circus. Heinreich's German Grill is your go-to spot for ice cream delights.

Sarasota Christian School gets high academic marks year after year, and the community of Gulf Gate is becoming a great family neighborhood. It used to be a retirement favorite. Now retirees are heading on over to the communities of Pine Shores and El Conquistador. El Conquistador has custom homes, a sports complex with golf and tennis, and is just minutes by foot to the Van Wezel performing Arts Hall. Sarasota is quite the diamond in the Central West area of Florida.

CENTRAL EAST REGION

This central area of Florida has more to offer than Disney and The Islands of Adventures. It also holds Cape Canaveral and the lovely city of New Smyrna Beach. It is also plentiful in lakes and rivers such as Lake Tohopekaliga, Halifax River, and the lovely Lake Louise.

Orlando traffic is horrendous during peak holiday dates as families flock to the numerous theme parks. However, the outer areas and townships are much easier to navigate. Cape Canaveral has a large military presence and New Smyrna is the smaller quieter sister of Daytona Beach. All have much to give the family and retiree looking to make a move to Florida.

ORLANDO
Climate

Since Orlando is in the center of the state, it does not get the cool ocean breezes that the coast is blessed with. The average temperatures for the year range from 60° to 85°. A theme park in 85-degree weather with no breeze can be a wilting experience. The high season is in the winter because of this reason, so while the lines are shorter in the summer, the heat is hot!

It has had four direct hurricane hits in the last fifty-four years, and all were doozies. In 1960, Hurricane Donna blew through, and in 2004, the trio of Charley, Frances, and Jeanne shook up the central east area.

History

The Disney history began in 1965, but as hard as it may be to believe, the city did exist before then. The city was born from the Seminole War in 1838 when the government built a fort of protection called Fort Gatlin.

Prior to the theme park boom, the entire area was covered with, citrus groves, orchards, cattle, and farmland. 1894 was remembered as the year the temperatures dropped into the 20° area and the entire citrus crop was lost.

In 1964, Disney began to quietly buy acreage. He had a plan and was laying the groundwork for the construction. He was very secretive as he did this, because the price was low and he didn't want the land price to skyrocket. The Disney opening was in 1971, and the Mickey mania began then and has never stopped!

Outdoor and Fun Entertainment Offerings

As a Florida resident, you are offered a discounted theme park pass, and you should get it. Buy it because all of your relatives will vacation with you from here on out, and you get to play tour guide!! There are approximately twenty theme parks in the area. Consider some of the less famous ones such as Aquatica and Discovery Cove. Additionally, your kids will want to go to Legoland many times!

There are quite a few sports' programs offering different leagues for the family, some are Athletics for Youth, Association of Christian

Youth Sports, and the City of Orlando Families, Parks, and Recreation.

At last count, there were 1111 houses of worship in the Orlando area. Many of them hold fall festivals where you can play games, enjoy the food, carve pumpkins and listen to music. The many lakes also provide boating and swimming fun.

Best Place for Young Families and Retirees to Live

The perimeter communities are best for families and for less traffic concerns. North Lake Park in Lake Nona has a school and a YMCA in the center of the community. Dr. Phillips community has wide sidewalks, green spaces, schools, and is home to the notorious Restaurant Row. It is located west of I-4.

The region is overflowing with retirement communities. The newest community for 55+ is called Gulfstream Harbor, Lakeshore Landings sits on a sapphire blue body of water, and Fairways Country Club has golf as a selling amenity feature.

Job Market

As you might expect, Disney World is the biggest employer with 55,000 employees. They also have a competitive internship that thousands of college students vie for every year. Orange County Public Schools employs close to the same amount of people; there are 54, 450 on their payroll. The well-known Florida Hospital has about 15,000 workers in their health care system.

Average Cost of Living:
- Consumer Price Index: 75.07
- Rent Index: 36.31
- Groceries Index: 86.84
- Restaurants Index: 60.59
- Consumer Price Plus Rent Index: 56.45

These scores are based out of 120. A score of 120 would be the most expensive place to live.

Places to Stay Away From

Stay away from Tangelo Park; it has a reputation as a base for drug dealers and drug shoppers. Also the west region of Interstate 4 as it weaves through the downtown area has a peak in muggings, violent, and sexual crimes. Most of Orlando is very, very safe for the crew.

CAPE CANAVERAL
Climate

There has never been a direct hit by a hurricane at Cape Canaveral. This is good news because the area dips a bit and it is prone to flooding. If a hurricane hits dead-on, the losses would be due to floodwaters, and they would be massive.

It never gets much cooler than mid-50s and usually tops out in heat near the high 80s. The lovely ocean breezes are exceptional in the winter and spring months.

History

In 1920, some Orlando residents purchased a large plot of land and began to develop the area. A family named the Brossiers, played a big role in developing the city of Cape Canaveral. They set aside several parks and public areas that still exist to this day. The idea was that everyone could enjoy this paradise adjacent to the ocean.

NASA arrived in 1958 and began to grow as the space program did. The area was selected for the implementation of over-the-water launces and for the warm year around temperatures.

Outdoor and Fun Entertainment Offerings

A NASA launch, landing, or planned activity would be great for the family to experience. If you tour the facility, plan on staying at least a full day. You can see some of the spaceships that have made history and go into some of the hangars. They also have an educational program for children.

The US Air Force has a space and missile museum in the area and it is free of charge. Just down the road at Cocoa Beach is the world famous Ron Jon Surf shop. Additionally, it you want to avoid the tourist type activities, the city has a full schedule of classes. They offer fun for the family such as dancing, karate, fitness camp, and yoga, boot camps. Patrick Air Force Base is located in Cape Canaveral and they have an extensive list of activities and events.

Best Place for Young Families and Retirees to Live

Due to NASA, Patrick Air Force Base, and the affordable homes in the area, there is a generous retiree population. Many of the retirees are military members. Indian River Colony Club is a 55+ community with a clubhouse, fitness center, golf course, tennis courts, and bike/hike trails. The prices range from $ 85,000.00 to $ 360,000.00.

Families might want to look at the Cape View neighborhood. The elementary school there has superior ratings. There are single-family homes as well as townhouses on the perimeter and the parks are plentiful. The school holds some community festivals and there are area pools for swimming.

Job Market

NASA and the base are the biggest employers. NASA has right at 18,000 employees. There is also a large fishing industry. Grouper, Cobia, Red Snapper, and Amberjacks are populous and the boats pull out for deep-sea fishing early each morning. Zilber Technology is rated as a good business to work for, and IAP Worldwide, a troop support company, hires often. There are other hospitality and tourist based jobs as well.

Average Cost of Living:
- Consumer Price Index: 76.97
- Rent Index: 37.91
- Groceries Index: 83.67
- Restaurants Index: 66.12
- Consumer Price Plus Rent Index: 58.21

Places to Stay Away From

The area just adjacent to the east I-95 is an area to avoid. There are also some deserted buildings on the backside (west) on US 1. Stay away from those spots, there is really no reason to be there, as they tend to have a higher crime rate. The rest of the city should be very safe for you and your family.

NEW SMYRNA BEACH

New Smyrna beach is a grid of sandy crisscrossed lanes that end at the ocean. The houses are welcoming with porches that gaze out toward the shores of the Atlantic.

Flagler Avenue is over 100 years old and the shops are mostly locally owned. They hold wine walks, art walks, have a Chowder festival, and hold Mardi Gras events. The sense of community is tremendous.

There are a number of private and public schools In New Smyrna Beach. Knight's Christian Academy and Glencoe Classical Academy regularly rank high in the academic performance in the state. Venetian Bay is west of the city proper and has parks, a clubhouse, a golf course, and a gated feature. It would be a great place for your family to live.

New Smyrna Beach advertises that is has 59 retirement communities within 60 miles of its city center. Quail Hollow is a manufactured retirement community with 241 homes. It is six miles from the beach and advertises dancing, dinners, a billiard's room, a laundry facility, as well as many other amenities.

SOUTHWEST REGION

The trees draped in Spanish moss that line the road to Captiva Island will wave a greeting to you as you wind and turn the curves. Naples has its own Fifth Avenue which is just as pricy and enticing as the one in NYC and the wooden quaint beach cottages of Fort Myers will remind you of times of the past. Lastly, a true find in the Southwest Naples area is Bonita Springs.

CAPTIVA ISLAND
Captiva Island is really an enclave for the rich. However, it is a spectacular island off the west coast of Florida. There is one way in the island, the Captiva Bridge. Buy a Sunpass for your tolls, so you are not always searching for change and dollars. You can order the Sun Pass online and use it all over Florida.

Once over the bridge, if you turn left you will go to Sanibel Island that has a great historic lighthouse. If you turn right (north), you are headed to Captiva Island. Once there, your life will never be the same.

Climate
In 2004, Hurricane Charley slammed into the 1.2-mile long island. The smaller north bridge washed out and there was no viable means of getting on to the north end for months. The yearly climate can dip in the 60° range and top out near

the high 90° in the summer. The ocean breezes are scrumptious to experience from a hammock under a palm tree.

History

Those to first live on Captiva were from the Calusa tribe around 3000 BC. Supposedly the name Captiva came from a pirate Jose Gaspar and his tendency to keep captives on the island. It is said that the first (and only for quite a while) modern inhabitant of Captiva Island was an Australian man named Binder.

Outdoor Fun Entertainment Offerings

This is the penultimate location for water lovers. You can swim, collect shells, fish, watch the manatees, see the dolphins run up and down the Gulf, and go boating. There is a bike path that runs the entire island length. Golf and tennis are also favorite pastimes.

Best Place for Young Families and Retirees to Live

The road to the end of the island (yes, there is one road) threads the Gulf and the bay. Along the road you will spy million dollar mansions and resorts. If I were going to live in Captiva whether I was in a young family or a retiree, I would select South Seas Plantation at the end of the island. The gated community has houses, villas, and condominiums. There are boats, restaurants, playgrounds, tennis courts, a golf court, an ice cream shop, and miles and miles of shoreline. You will not be able to buy there for under a million dollars (unless you are the luckiest person on the face of the earth). There are less expensive homes on other parts of the island and you can find condos in the $ 80,000-90,000 ranges. It is considered an ideal place for a second home.

Job Market
The jobs available on the island are teaching (The Sanibel/Captiva schools), shopping, fishing, and hospitality related.

Average Cost of Living
- Consumer Price Index: 76.99
- Rent Index: 87.87
- Groceries Index: 83.69
- Restaurants Index: 76.12
- Consumer Price Plus Rent Index: 88.20

Places to Stay Away From
The entire island is safe. Just keep an eye on the children since the area is surrounded by water.

NAPLES
For many years, Naples was the vacation and relocation spot for people from the Midwest. Now the entire country has discovered the beauty of Naples. The beaches are like sugar sand, the outlet shopping options are considered the best in the southeast, there is a local good sized airport, they have a 5th Avenue, and yet the pace is still slower than that of south east Florida.

Climate
The Naples area is considered a low risk for a hurricane hit. However, in 2005 Hurricane Wilma entered the state at Naples and then moved across the southeast portion of Florida. Naples does get a

fair amount of rain and it has some low-lying areas. Whenever you purchase a Florida home check the availability for flood insurance carefully. It is a must have for a Florida home. The temperatures run from the low 60° to the high 90°.

History

The Calusa or Caloosa tribe resided here back in 3000 BC. The waters and mild temperatures provide an excellent place to live and thrive. In the late 1860s, two men, Roger Gordon and Joe Wiggins, decided to make a settlement in the region.

The name comes from the fact that the temperature and life style in the early days was considered a mirror of Naples, Italy. The wealthy from Kentucky made the place their own in the 1870s. They were lead by newspaperman, Walter Halderman. He helped promote and build up the port and dock industry. You can tour some of his old dock warehouses that are now trendy shops. A piece of his pier still remains today.

The Naples hotel was a secret hideaway for movie stars in the 1900s. Barron Collier bought one million acres, mostly swampland, and began to develop the area. Tamiami Trail was built in 1923. Slowly, people have discovered the area. One of the best beaches in Florida is the small strip near the Ritz Carlton and Vanderbilt beach area. You can walk for an hour in ankle deep water and pick up shells as the dolphins roll by just out of reach.

Outdoor Fun Entertainment Offerings

Naples likes a good party. These parties usually take place in the downtown Fifth Avenue area. There are jazz, opera, and art festivals. Some of the many are the Film Festival, the Mullet Festival, and the Winter Wine Festival. Naples is also very serious about its high school football. You will find yourself in a stadium on fall Friday nights. Naples High School, and A rated academic school, usually does well in the playoffs.

Shopping, putt-putt, water sports, dog racing, golfing, and oodles of community events will fill your schedule. If you think you have absolutely nothing to do, situate yourself near a body of water, and alligator watch-you will see some.

Best Place for Young Families and Retirees to Live

Del Webb is a nice retirement location. It has single family and attached homes and the price range is $100,000.00-300,000.00. It is a +55 community.

For families, Autumn Woods and Reflection Lakes are nice gated communities. All of them have walking trails, pools, clubhouses, and play area for the kids. There is a wide range in pricing from $100,000.00 all the way to 600,000.00.

Autumn Woods has an activity director for knitting classes and things such as Rummikube competition games. It is located just over two miles from the Gulf of Mexico and near churches, the library, and local synagogues. It will be an ideal abode for a retiree or a family home.

Job Market

Naples is spread out some. So there is not one distinct area where the jobs will be found. Obviously there are retail and hospitality jobs, as well as outdoor sporting employment options. The biggest employers are:

- Lee County Memorial Health
- Lee County Public Schools
- Publix Stores
- Wal-Mart
- Target
- Florida Gulf Coat University

Average Cost of Living

- Consumer Price Index: N/V
- Rent Index: 52.93
- Groceries Index: N/V
- Restaurants Index: 73.08
- Consumer Price Plus Rent Index: N/V

Places to Stay Away From

Be wary as you travel in the Golden Gate and far east Naples area. There are some abandoned rentals and there is a slight spike in crime in those areas. The rest of Naples is very, very safe.

FORT MYERS

The beach houses on stilts, with wide porches, and a never-ending ocean view are one of the biggest drawing points of Fort Myers. Thomas Edison and Henry Ford liked the area so much they bought neighboring homes on the Caloosahatchee River.

Climate

The climate is similar to the other cities in the area. Fort Myers is also a very low strike area for hurricanes.

History

The army has a strong history in the area dating back to the 1830s. The Calusa and the Seminole tribes were a presence in the region. The actual incorporation of the city was in 1885. The waterways from the Gulf to the Intrcoastal as well as down and across the swamps made the area an ideal traffic way for the Confederate army during the Civil War.

Outdoor Fun Entertainment Offerings

The Fort Myers pier area is quite entertaining. There is music, cafes, water sport rentals, and lovely views. It has a very small town coastal feel. High school sports are big in Fort Myers and they hold an annual basketball classic called the City of Palms. If you want to see future college and NBA players, buy a ticket to attend.

The Edison Festival of Light, the 4th of July Celebrations, Fort Myers Shrimp Beach Festival, and Artfest are just a few local favorite fun festivals to be had. The sidewalks near the beach area are wide enough for biking and your daily run.

Job Market

Average Cost of Living
- Consumer Price Index: N/V
- Rent Index: 32.20

- Groceries Index: 72.10
- Restaurants Index: 62.63
- Consumer Price Plus Rent Index: N/V

Places to Stay Away From

The Tice, Ortiz Avenue, and Dunbar areas have an extremely high rate of crime compared to the rest of the region. Stay away from those areas.

BONITA SPRINGS

In the last ten years, Bonita Springs has grown enormously. It is located just a bit north of Naples. The major thoroughfares are Tamiami Trail and Interstate 75. There are scores of new communities being built at present. Finding your price range should not be difficult.

The population is around 50,000 and growing each day. People are attracted to the fine schools, affordable homes, and entertainment opportunities. Naples and Fort Myers airports are close by the city. The Coconut Point neighborhood is the best for families. Mirasol and Coconut Point has townhouse, single-family homes, and condominiums. The homes are in the low $200,000.00 range and Bonita Springs Charter School and Bonita Springs Middle Center for Arts are both within ten miles distance.

The friendly climate, many excursions, and affordable prices make Bonita Springs an ideal place for your new family home.

SOUTHEAST REGION

Miami is white hot just like its NBA team, the Heat. The areas around Miami are just as exciting and fun filled for both families and retirees. The varied communities are distinct, unique, and incredibly diverse in culture, cuisine, and lifestyle. Cities to the north like Plantation, Fort Lauderdale, and wonderful Wilton Manors are just as attractive in lifestyle and attraction options.

MIAMI
The layout of Miami can change with the simple turn of your car. You can live in style at South Beach, move west to larger properties in the Kendall or Cutler Bay area, or reside at the shores of Biscayne Bay. One description would never be sufficient for Miami, you would need fifty descriptions. Coconut Grove continues to attract families with fine schools like LaSalle High School and Ransom Everglades. Ransom Everglades sits on the water and for football games; they place an assistant in a rowboat to catch balls that go though the goal post! If you are interested in the Miami area, plan on spending three or four days just finding the neighborhood that suits you best.

Climate
Miami is a sultry tropical city. There may be a week or two of cool weather in the winter. Cool

weather in Miami is sixty and fifty degrees. The summer is the rainy season. Almost every afternoon the storms roll in and the thunder roars. Miami also gets a few brushes from hurricanes and tropical storms on occasion. Hurricane season runs from June to November 1.

History

Before the Spanish claimed Miami, the Tequestas tribe inhabited the region known as Biscayne Bay Country. This area was wild with brush, tickets, and rough terrain. Were it not for Julia Tuttle's impact on Henry Flagler, who knows if the area would have ever been cleared. But Flagler's railroad came and in 1896, the city was incorporated.

The city is known for so much: Al Capone, Wet-Foot/Dry-Foot, hanging chads in the presidential election, Elian Gonzalez, South Beach, LeBron James, Gloria Estevez, the Versace killing, Dan Marino, the 90 riots, the Graham family, and Hurricane Andrew. The history is just as rich and diverse as the population of Miami.

Outdoor Fun Entertainment Offerings

There are many outdoor fun activities, and most cities have a well-developed sports program, such as PAL. Attending the Miami Heat games can be exciting, but very expensive. On the other hand, the Marlins are also thrilling, but the tickets are very affordable. Additionally, the Miami Dolphins are located on the Dade and Broward County border. Water sports abound and boating excursions can be had any day of the week. There are festivals such as The Renaissance Festival at

Vizcaya mansion or the Coconut Grove Festival. For celebrity watching, go to Joe's Stone Crab in South Beach and enjoy stone crabs and seeing the famous stars. Afterwards you could catch the Miami City ballet for your cultural experience. You may have a hard time picking what activity you want to do since the choices are so vast.

Best Place for Young Families and Retirees to Live

Because each community is so unique and because each one has homes and lifestyles suitable for retirees and for young families, this is a personal call. Coconut Grove does have it all: the water, condominiums, townhouses, apartments, homes, shopping, festivals, good schools, a strong sense of community, and restaurants.

Job Market

There are many job opportunities in Miami. Big employers are the Miami Heat, Miami Dolphins, Florida Marlins, Dade County School System, Miami International Airport, The Miami Herald, and any job in the water sports or hospitality fields.

Average Cost of Living
- Consumer Price Index: 83.45
- Rent Index: 56.44
- Groceries Index: 90.42
- Restaurants Index: 76.64
- Consumer Price Plus Rent Index: 70.48

Places to Stay Away From

Miami can turn ugly fast. Million dollar homes back up to US 1, the airport perimeter has a large homeless population, and Overtown is just now becoming a proud and historic community again. Be very vigilant when you are downtown, around US 1, anywhere near the Miami River, and as you get close to Interstate-95. Always know where you purse, possessions, and car are located. Be smart when in Miami.

PLANTATION

To the west of Fort Lauderdale and to the east of the Everglades sits a very family friendly community known as Plantation. One of the top ten private schools in the nation, American Heritage, is on Broward Boulevard in Plantation. There are hundreds of family communities, houses with large tracts, swimming pools galore, and a plethora of temples, synagogues, mosques, and churches.

Climate

The climate is similar to Miami's climate. It does get toasty in the tropics. Parts of Plantation are prone to flooding as was discovered when Hurricane Wilma roared through the city in 2005. There is an elaborate system of canals that runs from the Atlantic Ocean to the Everglades, and straight through Plantation. As a result many homes back to a canal, and iguanas and alligators are common sights.

History

Plantation is relatively new as far as Florida cities go. Mr. Peters founded it in the early 1930s. The original and existing draw for the city is the large tracts of land that come with many properties. The city was actually incorporated in 1953, with a mere population of 500 people. The city motto is "Out of wilderness, this city."

Outdoor Fun Entertainment Offerings

Football and girls' soccer rule at the high school level in Plantation, Florida. Make sure to stop by and watch a game. Fishing and swimming are abundant. Just five minutes south is a cowboy friendly community called Davie and you can go attend the rodeo. For food and shopping fun check out the The Hard Rock Casino which is located just south of the city. The Seminole tribe owns the resort and has a varied cultural schedule of events at the outdoor arena at the casino. Central Park public park system has tennis courts, pools, many fields, and an active PAL program. This is a very family friendly city.

Best Place for Young Families and Retirees to Live

Planation Acres and Jacaranda are the two best locales for young families to consider. Plantation Acres is zoned for horses and Jacaranda has a private country club with clubhouse and restaurant. Both are located in the West Broward Boulevard area. Covenant Village on Broward Boulevard is an active and prestigious retirement community.

Job Market

The Sawgrass Outlet Mall has thousands of employees and open positions. The Broward County School system hires often for the Plantation public schools, and Suncoast marketing is a big employer in Plantation.

Average Cost of Living

- Consumer Price Index: 76.99
- Rent Index: 37.87
- Groceries Index: 83.69
- Restaurants Index: 66.12
- Consumer Price Plus Rent Index: 58.20

Places to Stay Away From

Plantation is very safe. There is a tiny strip just east of US 441 that could be considered a tiny bit unsafe. Other than that, the region is quite secure.

FORT LAUDERDALE

Fort Lauderdale is Miami's little sister. Shop on Las Olas Avenue, ride on the Jungle Queen Riverboat, go to the Discovery Center or the Broward Performing Arts Center, and then have dinner at famous Foxy Brown's all in one day. The prices in the area are high. Paradise and a good pair of sunglasses do not come cheaply.

Climate

The climate is very tropical. Expect a few scares from tropical storms or hurricanes every few years, and the rainy season is June to August. December is a lovely time in Fort Lauderdale. You can open your windows and take advantage of the breezes and milder temperatures. Holiday decorations are plentiful and you see people driving around in convertibles checking out the light displays.

History

Fort Lauderdale is named after General Lauderdale. While local tribes and the Spanish inhabited the city, it is probably best known for Annette Funicello, Frankie Avalon, and Spring break. Very few college kids vacation for spring break in Fort Lauderdale these days though the Elbow Room is still operating.

Outdoor Fun Entertainment Offerings

The beach and water are big. The city is known as the Venice of America. Lauderdale by the Sea has Friday fun nights where they block the area off by the ocean and have food and music. The pier is located at the end of Commercial Boulevard and the fishing is ripe. There are a thousand festivals and many outdoor concerts. Holiday Park does an outdoor summer concert series and outdoor movies take place at Fort Lauderdale Beach in the summer. The beach traffic in season, which is late November to March, is horrendous.

Best Place for Young Families and Retirees to Live

Coral Ridge community would suffice for both retirees and young families. Small condos and apartments dot the perimeter of the community. Inside the community are single-family homes. Christ Church and St. John the Baptist are in the community directly beside a lovely public park. Both religious facilities have schools. Christ Church serves grades K-8 and Cardinal Gibbons Catholic School serves grades 9-12. The community is adjacent to shops, grocery stores, and the beach.

Job Market

Holy Cross Hospital and Imperial Point Hospital are big employers. There are a thousand law offices downtown, and the Fort Lauderdale International Airport hires many people. The port, restaurant, hospitality, and water sporting business have many spots. AutoNation, an 11 million dollar enterprise, has a large work pool.

Average Cost of Living
- Consumer Price Index: 84.13
- Rent Index: 46.74
- Groceries Index: 86.04
- Restaurants Index: 71.12
- Consumer Price Plus Rent Index: 66.17

Places to Stay Away From

US 1 to the west is not a very desirable area. Sistrunk area has a high crime rate and parts of Andrews Avenue and Pompano Beach neighborhoods are crime-ridden. Just like in Miami, in Fort Lauderdale the areas can go bad fast. Always, always know where you are and be vigilant.

WILTON MANORS

Wilton Manors is a lovely hamlet known for its acceptance of absolutely everyone. This area is in the region west of Fort Lauderdale. The homes are older and quite quaint and there are a number of apartments and condominiums. Take the children to high tea at Oscar's Tea Room and then go next door at paint at Painting with a Twist. The local public school is called Wilton Manors Elementary. The two parks in the area, Colohatchee and Richardson Park, both have an active agenda. There are a number of retirement organizations such as Independence Hall. Visit Wilton Manors, it will steal your heart.

THE FLORIDA KEYS

After Florida City, the top Florida Key is Key Largo. There is one way into the Keys, US 1. On your right you can see the waters of the Gulf and on your left you can see the Atlantic Ocean.

There is a Crocodile Crossing sign about half way to Key West. Apparently the crocodiles have been known to drift over from South America.

Each Key is a bit different. Key Largo, Marathon Key, and Key West are all tropical paradises that would make a great spot for your new home if you love the sun, sand, and sea.

Please note that there were no cost of living statistics available for the Keys. The money you would spend depends on the lifestyle you select. From the standpoint of real estate, there is everything from million dollar beach houses, trailers, condos, studio apartments, and conch cottages.

History
Flagler's railroad opened the Keys up to the world. Its original name was Cayo Largo, which means Long Key. The Key was made famous by the Key Largo movie, but very little of the movie was actually filmed here.

Family Life with Children
Are the South Florida Keys a place for families, including young children and teens? The

answer, perhaps surprisingly for those unfamiliar with this area, is an enthusiastic "yes." As long as you're fully aware the Keys reflect an "island life" and are sort of "off the beaten path" then it can still be a very nice place to raise a family.

There are twelve public schools in the Keys. There are three public high schools: Coral Shores, Key West HS, and Marathon HS. There are also eight private schools including: Island Christian (Islamaroda, serves PK-12), Keys Academy of Science (in Key Largo, serves K-9) and Mary Immaculate (in Key West, serves PK-8).

There are no big malls in the Keys (beyond the strip mall), but there are marinas, beach and boating clubs, sailing groups, scuba and snorkeling events. (Key kids don't really hang out at the mall). This, in essence, is why it would be a good place for many to raise a family. Your child's playground can be the ocean in the Keys.

KEY LARGO
Climate
This is the Florida tropics. There are warm days, warmer days, and hotter than you can imagine days. Oddly enough, hurricanes have stayed away from the Keys for years. But the consideration that there is only one way out of town if a hurricane does hit is something you need to know.

Outdoor Fun Entertainment Opportunities
There are quite a few outdoor attractions. If you and your family scuba dive, you can dive the Spiegel Wreck. Key Largo likes to advertise itself as the Diving Capital of the World. The

Everglades National Park has 1.4 million acres where you can see alligators, birds, bobcats, and deer.

There is a pool complex called Jacobs Aquatic Center. Jacobs offers lessons and camps. The replica African Queen is in Key Largo and well as Hemingway's famous boat the Pilar. Additionally, you can swim, boat, and fish in Key Largo.

Best Place for Young Families and Retirees to Live

There is a retirement community in Key Largo called Silver Shores. It has a pool, boat pier and dockage, tennis courts, and a community clubhouse. Any location would be ideal for a young family. Roads branch off from the Overseas Highway and down each of these lanes are beautiful houses close to the waters.

Job Market

If you want to work on the water, this is the spot for you. Here are a lot of marinas with openings for body workers, painters, and mechanics. The many restaurants and tourist attractions hire a lot of people. Mariner's Hospital is located just south of Key Largo and employs 250 people.

Places to Stay Away From

The most dangerous places in Key Largo is the two-lane highway when it backs up on weekends and of course, always watch the kids around all this water.

MARATHON KEY

Marathon is a middle Key known for its seven-mile long bridge. The Key is actually only ten miles long. It is a boating mecca with over 1,200 dry boat slips and 1,200 wet boat slips. Marathon has a small airport for personal and small plane use.

Climate

The ocean breezes are divine, but Key temperatures can hit the 100° mark in the summer. Sell your coats and sweaters and invest in flip-flops and swim trunks.

History

Marathon had an early Spanish presence as was originally known as Key Vaca. Vaca means cow and this name refers to the sea cow or the manatee. In the mid-1800s, the area was a ship building location. Flagler's Overseas railroad came to the area in the late 1800s. You can still see remnants of the old railroad, which was washed out by a hurricane, standing in the Atlantic Ocean.

Outdoor Fun Entertainment Opportunities

Crane Point Museum is a preserved hardwood grove with an early 20th Century home on the property. Tours and hikes are given at Crane Point. You and your family can snorkel, dive, sail, or attend the local marine education center. Some favorite reefs are Delta Shoals, Sombrero Reef, and Coffin Patch. The Marathon Seafood Festival takes place in the spring every year.

Best Place for Young Families and Retirees to Live

Marathon Key has quite a few manufactured home communities with an active agenda for young families or for retirees. Some of them are Galway Bay, Ocean Breeze, and Pelican Carefree Resort.

Job Market

All of the Keys are going to have jobs relative to water sports, hospitality, and marinas. There are three pubic schools in Marathon, Florida. The Dade County School system operates the schools and they are a large employer in the area.

Places to Stay Away From

The traffic and no-see-ums (tiny mosquitos) are the most dangerous things to watch out for in Marathon Key.

KEY WEST

Key West is known for Hemingway, key lime pies, the historical lighthouse, amazing seafood, and laid back island attitude that will have you singing Jimmy Buffet songs before you know it.

Climate

The temperatures range from the 70° to the 100° mark. There are lovely breezes and the occasional afternoon rain shower. Statistics indicate that Key West has some sort of effect from tropical storms every three years. These effects of late have been strong winds or rain. Hurricane Isaac last affected it in 2005.

History

Key West has a Spanish history. But the history of the city is built on the back of pirates and wreck thieves. When a ship would run aground, the city bell would ring, and sailors would boat to the wreck. The first one there got to claim it and keep the ship's goods. Many a ship has wrecked in the area around Key West. The city famously tired to secede from the union in 1995 as the newly formed Conch Republic.

Outdoor Fun Entertainment Opportunities

Key West is fun, and despite what you may have heard, it is family friendly. Go on the local ghost tour, watch the sunset as you walk to Mallory Square and watch the Catman and his performing felines, shop on Duval, eat outside at My Blue Heaven (Hemingway used to box there), climb the light house, tour the Little white House, go to an art gallery, visit the Pirate's museum, or tour Hemingway's home. There is more to do than you will ever have time for. And by all means take a trolley tour of the town!

Best Place for Young Families and Retirees to Live

There are quite a few nice family style homes in the area across from Key West High School. The Old Towne is magnetic with its historic cottages, lush gardens, and sidewalks for strolling. You can smell the ocean and dip into it after a long day of work. There are also a large amount of houseboats that might be considered as an alternative way of life.

Job Market

Key West jobs are not you normal run of the meal jobs. You could be a ghost tour guide, a performer at Mallory Square, a tattoo artist, a mime, a rickshaw driver, drive a trolley, or a become a hawker for time-share units. If these jobs are too extreme for you, there are educational, service, water, and hospitality jobs.

Places to Stay Away From

The Bahamian area can get scary at night. Additionally there is an area on the west side of Whitehead Street that has run down houses and a high crime rate. Free roam chickens and cats are all over the city; if either animal scares you, keep an eye out for them.

CONCLUSION

Well, my dear reader, that about sums things up. As stated at the beginning of this book, I set out to genuinely present a complete picture of Florida so you could make a truly informed decision about whether or not moving here would be right for you.   I certainly hope you feel like I delivered on my promise.

Moving to Florida is the right choice for many individuals.   It fulfills their expectations in ways few other places could ever match.

Just remember that even if Florida (as a location) is right for you, it's still important to come here on the right terms – your terms. Logistical planning will help put you in the best financial position, before and after coming here. And considering the relationships you now enjoy with family and friends, in whatever state you'd be moving from, will help you anticipate the changes in your personal life that would inevitably come after such a move.

Now, are you ready for an adventure in your life? Is Florida going to be a part of it? Whatever you choose, I wish you the very best!

May your days be filled with sunshine. May a warm ocean caress your toes. And may your life

Conclusion

be filled with joy ... whether you find yourself in Florida as a full-time resident ... or a part-time visitor. May Florida be for you what is truly best for you.

Best Places to Live in Florida

Your guide for finding the best place to live in Florida today ...

Includes cities / towns ideal for singles, couples, families & retirees

Dagny Wasil

CPSIA information can be obtained
at www.ICGtesting.com
Printed in the USA
BVOW11s1126040118
504323BV00001B/10/P